the smart approach to®

home
RENOVATION

CRE&TIVE
HOMEOWNER®

the smart approach to®

home

RENOVATION

Susan Boyle Hillstrom

CREATIVE HOMEOWNER®, Upper Saddle River, New Jersey

THE SMART APPROACH TO® HOME RENOVATION

SENIOR EDITOR	Kathie Robitz
SENIOR DESIGNER	Glee Barre
PHOTO RESEARCHER	Stan Sudol
EDITORIAL ASSISTANT	Jennifer Calvert
INDEXER	Schroeder Indexing Services
COVER DESIGN	Glee Barre
FRONT COVER PHOTOGRAPHY	(both) Mark Samu, design: Lucianna Samu
INSIDE FRONT COVER PHOTOGRAPHY	(top) Mark Samu; (bottom) Bruce McCandless/CH
BACK COVER PHOTOGRAPHY	(top and inset) Mark Samu; (center) melabee m miller; (bottom and inset) Mark Samu
INSIDE BACK COVER PHOTOGRAPHY	(top) Mark Samu; (bottom) Jessie Walker

CREATIVE HOMEOWNER

VP/EDITORIAL DIRECTOR	Timothy O. Bakke
PRODUCTION MANAGER	Kimberly H. Vivas
ART DIRECTOR	David Geer
MANAGING EDITOR	Fran J. Donegan

Current Printing (last digit)
10 9 8 7 6 5 4 3 2

The Smart Approach to® Home Renovation, First Edition
Library of Congress Control Number: 2006931866
ISBN-10: 1-58011-303-6
ISBN-13: 978-1-58011-303-8

CREATIVE HOMEOWNER®
A Division of Federal Marketing Corp.
24 Park Way
Upper Saddle River, NJ 07458
www.creativehomeowner.com

acknowledgments

I hope this book will be helpful to all who read it. If it is, it will be thanks to the many people who helped put it together.

Many thanks to Kathie Robitz, a talented and supportive editor, and to the design staff at Creative Homeowner, who made a beautiful book.

I'm also grateful to Mark Samu for patiently enduring so many interviews— and for taking great pictures—and to Lucianna Samu for her fabulous sense of design. Thanks also to N'ann Harp of Smart Consumer Services, Elaine Petrowski, Jeffrey Hartt, Deirdre Gatta, The Donnellys, The McGrails, and my wonderful husband, Roger Hillstrom.

contents

introduction

Everyone has heard remodeling horror stories across the back fence or over dinner with friends. Never mind. Your experience does not have to be nightmarish. *The Smart Approach to® Home Renovation* has the advice you need for planning and financing the project, hiring the right professionals, and preparing your house for the onslaught of a work crew so that your project can have a happy ending.

See how real people tackled their own remodeling projects: kitchens, baths, additions, exterior makeovers, and outdoor living areas. Their experiences, as presented here, will inspire you with ideas for renovations of your own and help you to focus those ideas into doable projects. Careful perusals of each Case Study and Design Workbook, including before and after photos, will show you how important it is to do your homework before you begin—a sure way to success.

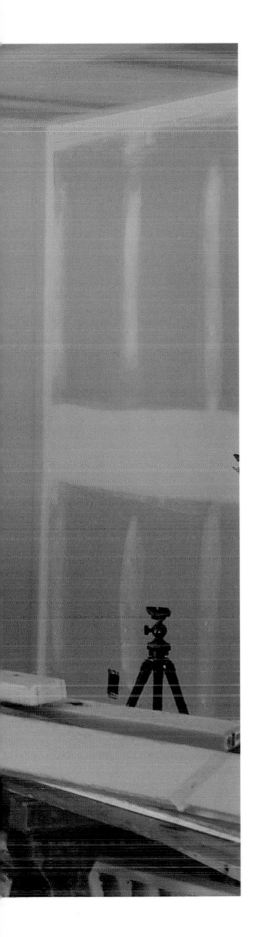

1

ready to remodel?

KNOW WHAT YOU'RE GETTING INTO   DO A SMART SEARCH
INTERVIEW MORE THAN ONE PROFESSIONAL   DIG DEEP

Before you take a single step toward fulfilling your remodeling dreams, do a thorough reality check. Sure, more than a million makeovers are done every year, but is remodeling right for you? A carefully planned, well-executed remodel will improve the livability and attractiveness of your home—and that is the best reason to undertake one. Certain projects will improve the resale value of your home, allowing you to recoup some or all of your remodeling dollars; but in most circumstances you need to sell within a year to reap that benefit. Some remodels detract from the resale value—pools, spas, tennis courts, and extreme decorative statements to mention a few. But if one of these makeovers will improve your lifestyle, you have made a good investment for yourself and your family. If you can afford it, forge ahead and enjoy the results.

Will a remodel improve your quality of life or the resale value of your home? Better still—will it do both?

Like all general rules, this one includes exceptions. If your home is small for its neighborhood and in need of improvement, updating style and quality could make financial sense, particularly if you keep costs reasonable. In this scenario, you can expect the market value of your home to exceed the cost of the remodel, even if you don't sell for several years.

know what you're getting into

Assess the financial viability of the remodel you're planning. To do this, you need two pieces of information. The first is the amount your house is worth in the current market. Get a ballpark figure from a local real-estate agent or a house appraiser. While you're at it, ask for an informed opinion about whether the type of remodel you plan is likely to increase the value of your property.

Knowing the value of your home will also help you calculate how much money to sink into a renovation. Many experts

suggest that 20 to 30 percent of your home's value is acceptable—more than that is risky. According to the National Association of the Remodeling Industry (NARI), it makes good sense to spend as much as necessary to create your dream house if you are planning to live there for another five years or more—and of course, if you can afford it. On the other hand, if you're planning to move soon, updating to neighborhood standards makes better sense. An online survey of 2,000 real-estate agents conducted by HomeGain's Home Sale Maximizer indicates that minor improvements such as painting inside or out, laying new floors or carpets, and upgrading electrical or plumbing systems actually yield the highest returns in terms of payback. And remember that over improving is not smart—make your house

BELOW
A master bedroom update will make your house more appealing to a future buyer. A cozy little fireplace ups the ante.

OPPOSITE
An attic renovation with a focus on low-maintenance materials produced this easy-care, multifunctional family room.

fancier and more expensive than surrounding ones and you will price it right out of the market and recover very little of your initial investment.

The second piece of information you need is the approximate cost of your proposed remodeling. There are a couple of ways to find out. Ask friends and neighbors who have had similar work done approximately what they paid; if you don't press them for an exact figure, they may be willing to ballpark it for you. Another approach—quiz your local building-code officer about the average cost per square foot of new construction in your area. (House appraisers and real-estate people might also have this information.) Then do some math—multiply that figure by the square footage of the improvements you plan to make, whether it's an addition or an update of existing space. To factor in the cost of finish carpentry, double that figure. Then add the costs of any equipment, surfaces, or finishes you plan to add, such as flooring, countertops, appliances, lighting, plumbing fixtures, paint, and wallpaper. The resulting figure will give you a rough, but helpful, idea of what you can expect to pay.

You might also ask a contractor for a rough idea of the costs. Unless he or she is the contractor you plan to use, make it clear that you are not ready to hire anyone. You're not asking for a bid—just a ballpark figure. If there's a small fee for this service, it's well worth it.

Equipped with these two pieces of information, you can assess the financial feasibility of your project. If your house is worth, say, $200,000 in the current market and the makeover will cost from $50,000 to $75,000 yet it will add $50,000 to its selling price within the next year or so, it makes sense. If it will take extensive—and expensive—changes to revamp your house to your liking, it may be cheaper and more satisfying in the long run to buy another house.

smart tip   REMODEL OR MOVE?

Before you do anything to your existing house, ask yourself the following questions:

- Do you like your present location?
- Is your house fundamentally sound? Do you like its style and layout?
- Can you afford to remodel?

- Will a remodel increase the value of the house? (It probably will unless it becomes too pricey for its neighborhood.)
- Will the family easily tolerate living with a remodeling? If not, do you have the wherewithal to live elsewhere while the work proceeds?
- Can you get more house for the money in another area that you like as well?

Don't Go It Alone

The kinds of remodelings we cover in this book are complex, incorporating some or all of the following—significant structural alterations, electricity and plumbing, cabinet and appliance installation, surfacing materials, and more. Depending on the size and scope of your own project, you may need the services of an architect, interior designer, kitchen or bath specialist, or a landscape designer.

ABOVE
Enlisting a kitchen specialist may help you get a kitchen that is as good-looking as it is efficient. Plus, you'll get the biggest bang for your remodeling buck.

RIGHT
Sun-space add-ons are popular remodeling projects. This addition provides a light-filled spot for relaxing, entertaining, and casual family meals, whatever the season.

■ **Architects.** A licensed professional trained in the art and science of building design, an architect will transform your ideas and dreams into an actual room or building that adheres to local codes and regulations. Architects often oversee an entire remodeling project, obtaining construction bids, selecting contractors and subcontractors, negotiating contracts, controlling the money, and handling any problems that come up. This kind of coverage is, of course, pricey—it will run you about 5 to 10 percent of the gross construction cost—but worth it for a large project that involves significant structural alterations. For a small project, you might hire an architect to create a design for your remodeling project and supply a set of working plans for the contractor.

■ **Interior Designers.** These people handle space planning and specifications for non-load-bearing interior construction, advising clients on the functionality and overall look of the room and suggesting the colors, finishes, furniture, fabrics, and other decorative details that pull it all together. You may want to work with an interior designer if your makeover will entail significant cosmetic changes.

■ **Certified Kitchen and Bath Designers.** Qualified by the National Kitchen and Bath Association (NKBA), these professionals are familiar with all elements of kitchen and bath design—layout, appliances, fixtures and fittings, surfacing materials, and decorative finishing touches.

■ **Design-Build Remodeling Firms.** These firms retain both designers and remodelers on staff, making them one-stop shops for design and construction services. This approach is generally less expensive than an architect-supervised job, and more expensive than hiring a contractor only. Many people prefer design-build firms because the necessary services are handled by a single company—if something goes wrong you have to make only one phone call.

RIGHT AND OPPOSITE

A family-room addition offers more than extra living space if you use it as an opportunity to reconfigure an existing layout by opening up the main floor of the house. Here, an open contemporary floor plan was created for an easy transition between the kitchen, family, game rooms (pictured), and other parts of the house.

■ **Landscape Architects.** Like building architects, these specialists produce three-dimensional solutions to space problems—but they do it outside the house, creating outdoor spaces, planting areas, and garden structures that are functional, pleasing to the eye, and in harmony with both the building and the site.

■ **General Contractors.** A good general contractor is skilled in all aspects of the remodeling trade and will be in charge of the project—unless you have hired an architect to oversee it—

establishing the schedule; ordering the building supplies, including appliances, fixtures, and surfacing materials; hiring and supervising a crew of subcontractors; and securing building permits and arranging inspections.

If your project is small and simple and you have great confidence in your own space-planning and design abilities, you may not need anyone but a contractor. But for a large remodeling, you'll probably be happier with the results if you use the expert-

LEFT
Outdoor makeovers are important, too. Let a garden designer or landscape architect create a soothing alfresco retreat for you.

ABOVE
A qualified and experienced general contractor can handle most aspects of a remodeling project—from painting to carpentry to the installation of doors, windows, cabinets, and appliances.

ise of an architect or designer. "Most general contractors don't provide design services," says N'ann Harp, president of Smart Consumer Services, a Burnside, North Carolina, consumer education and assistance organization that specializes in homeowner-contractor relationships. "If you ask your contractor for design advice, he or she will likely suggest what's easiest to build."

Another possibility is to do the job yourself or entrust it to the purported DIY skills of friends or relatives. Unless you are doing a cosmetic update of a room or adding a simple deck, this is a risky proposition. You might save money initially, but any mistakes you make will come back and haunt you, in both money and anguish. However, some homeowners handle DIY jobs well. Take the quiz on page 31 to see if you are one of them.

Proceed with care as you find, select, and hire a pro. Remodeling is stressful even when it goes smoothly. Don't magnify the stress by hiring unreliable people who do shoddy work.

smart steps
do your homework

■ Step 1 DO A SMART SEARCH

Thinking of restricting your search for a reliable professional to the Yellow Pages? Think again. A splashy ad may indicate that an architect, designer, or contractor has some money to spend—and it will often spell out their areas of expertise, which is helpful—but it is no guarantee of professionalism, skill, or experience. Membership in trade or professional associations may indicate that a professional has met certain industry standards, and these associations are handy for steering you toward likely candidates in your area. (See the Resource Guide for a list of these associations.)

You'll also find candidates in the home section of your local newspaper and in design magazines that highlight the work of a professional near you. Many websites list names of remodeling contractors in your vicinity; but take with a large grain of salt the claim that these people have been "prescreened." Always do your own research.

The best way to find a reliable professional is through the recommendations of friends, neighbors, or coworkers who have recently done remodelings similar to the project you are planning—provided that you ask these people the right questions and look at the finished job itself.

Don't settle for a general recommendation, no matter how glowing. Ask for details: Did the professionals keep appointments? Were they easy to work with? Were they respectful of your ideas? Did they adhere to the schedule? Did they stay with the job until it was completely finished? Would you wholeheartedly recommend them?

If possible, take a close look at the project itself, whether finished or in progress, looking for such details as sturdy framing and subflooring, smooth and seamless drywall, neat carpentry and paint jobs with no gaps or visible brush strokes. Scrutinize finished floors—you shouldn't see nails, unevenness, or cupping. If the job is in progress, stay out of the way while you assess the following—does it seem to be progressing smoothly; is the site clean and orderly; does the quality of work appear to be good?

LEFT
Even minor changes can improve household efficiency. This once-dreary space now blooms as a crisp, plant-filled laundry and mudroom. Easy-to-clean tile is a smart choice for flooring.

BEFORE

AFTER

ABOVE AND RIGHT
Simple but effective—some creamy-white paint, a refinished wood floor, and an eye-catching light fixture transformed this entrance hall from bland and boring to spectacular and welcoming. The remodeling budget was small, but the impact is great. Tackling another small project with a big payoff, the homeowners converted a closet at the end of the hallway into a small additional bathroom.

Step 2 INTERVIEW MORE THAN ONE PROFESSIONAL IN EACH CATEGORY

Follow this advice even if you think you've already made up your mind. If nothing else, these interviews may give you some ideas and approaches to your project that you hadn't thought of. If you're going to use an architect or designer, interview people in those categories before you go on to contractors and conduct the interviews at the job site if possible. It's not essential that the people you hire become your new best friends, but effective communication and mutual respect are important. If you feel ill at ease or detect a condescending or dismissive attitude toward your ideas and vision, beware.

Ask to see portfolios. Don't worry if you don't love every example of an architect's or designer's work, but if all of them represent a big departure from your tastes and preferences, it could lead to conflict. If your dream is a clean-lined contemporary space and the pro shows you page after page of fussy country-style projects, you may want to look for someone who is comfortable working in more than one style.

BEFORE

ABOVE AND OPPOSITE
Earth tones in a new checkerboard-patterned wood floor blend beautifully with the creamy walls and rattan furniture in this family room. The homeowner did the work himself, applying a translucent stain in the lighter squares so that the wood grain shows.

smart tip BIDS

The ideal bid allows a fair price for the homeowners and a reasonable profit for the contractor.

■ Give each contractor a copy of your plans and specs. That way, all candidates are bidding on the same thing.

■ Beware of very low bids. They may indicate a poor estimator or, worse, a contractor who hopes to compensate later by instituting change orders or substituting cheaper materials. For this reason bids should specify types and brands of all materials to be used. If this information is not in writing, it can be changed without your knowledge.

■ View very high bids with caution, too. Many experts believe that a 15-percent gap between a homeowner's budget and a contractor's bid is too much. But don't reject the high-bidding contractor out of hand—instead, see if you can close the gap by making changes in the scope of the job or the materials.

At this point, ask a couple of questions—how long have you been in business (the longer, the better); how many projects like mine have you done; what, roughly, would you charge for the project? It's too soon for an actual estimate, but a rough figure will tell you if you and your candidates are in the same ballpark. Having done your homework, you will know about how much you can spend. A gap of more than 15 percent between what you have budgeted and what the pro expects to be paid is too great, say experts. If that occurs, look elsewhere or be prepared to trim your budget.

Help the pros you interview calculate an approximate fee by being very specific. Don't say, "I want to update my kitchen," but, "I want to gut the kitchen; replace all cabinets, appliances, and surfaces; and lay the room out differently." Not, "Build me an addition," but, "Add

AFTER

a two-story space to the rear of the house with a family room that opens to the kitchen on the first floor and a bedroom and bath on the second floor."

According to N'ann Harp of Smart Consumer Services, most homeowners fail to have a firm design and budget in mind when they start a project. "They wrongly imagine that they'll 'get more' out of a contractor if they keep their plans and budget somewhat secret," she says. "But the clearer the owners' grasp of what they want and what it should cost, the better."

At this point in the interview, ask for at least three references. Ask candidates to show you their contractor's license, if your state government requires one, and insurance certificates; and make a note of the policy numbers and the insurer's name. All contractors should have current liability insurance and worker's compensation.

A word about legal issues: anytime you enter into an agreement you are also entering the legal world of a litigious society. As one of the contractual parties, you have certain rights. For example, under the right of recision you can change your mind within three days of signing a contract without any liability, provided the contract was signed some place other than the designer or contractor's office—at your home, for example. This grace period protects you against hasty decisions and hard sells. Federal law mandates that consumers be made aware of the right to cancel a contract without penalty. Ask your design professional or contractor about it.

You may also request waivers of lien, which release you from liabilities for subcontractors and manufacturers. At the end of the job, ask for a final lien waiver for each person who worked on the project: this will protect you from third-party debts and obligations. It's also a good idea to ask your contractor for a signed affidavit stating that all subcontractors have been compensated, a protection against having to pay twice

because your contractor didn't make good on his debts. With a lien waiver you can refer an unpaid subcontractor to the general contractor for payment.

Furthermore, do not allow any work to be done on your property that is not detailed in writing. If you want to change something, get a written change order. And remember any change, whether initiated by you or by a supplier or vendor, will cost more money. Every change order should describe what is to be done, how much it will cost, and what impact it will have, if any, on the project schedule.

■ Step 3 DIG DEEP

Previous customers can give invaluable information about the professionals you are considering. Most people are happy to talk about their experience, good or bad.

Don't stop, however, after just one positive or negative reference. For a balanced picture, call all three and focus on performance rather than personality. A bad

report may be the result of a personality conflict—don't reject a potentially reliable person on the basis of one complaint. Check further.

The same is true with the results of calls to the Better Business Bureau and your state consumer-affairs agency, calls you should definitely make. Don't focus only on the complaints filed against a candidate; look also to see if the conflicts have been satisfactorily resolved. While you're making calls, verify the status of the contractor's license and be sure insurance coverage is current. Do not allow uninsured workers to place themselves in hazardous situations in and around your home. And you might check out your own liability, too—your insurance agent may suggest that you adjust your homeowner's coverage during the project.

A Cautionary Tale

Magda and her husband, Sam (not their real names), thought they did everything right when they hired a contractor to do a major remodel of their suburban house. "He came recommended by the architect," says Magda. "He had insurance, business cards, and letterheads; his trucks and shirts sported matching logos. But we didn't leave it at that. We did Better Business Bureau research, asked for references, checked references, and signed a lengthy contract."

Even so, the couple quickly found themselves in a remodeling hell that lasted for more than a year. The contractor broke ground in April, Magda reports, and then worked off and on until November, leaving his second-in-command in charge most of the time. The second-in-command didn't have a strong work ethic either, the couple eventually discovered: he would show up in the morning and work for about 45 minutes, until the homeowners left for work; then he'd pack up and leave, too. "The only reason the contractor started working regular days," Magda says, "is that I freaked out, came back home one day with a camera, and told the second-in-command that I was taking pictures for the judge."

The couple finally fired this contractor from hell and found somebody else. There is still some work to be done, but they have temporarily run out of money. And yes, they are suing the contractor.

So what went wrong? Looking back, Magda says she would do a few things differently, such as the way she checked references. "It's the ones who don't call back that speak volumes,"

LEFT AND ABOVE
Be prepared—remodelings are messy and create lots of dust, dirt, and debris. Whether you're doing the work yourself or relying on professionals, you'll need to set aside one or more rooms to serve as a serene retreat from the noise and clutter.

she says. "I got eight or nine references, but three or four of those people never called me back even though I called them several times. Now I know they were saying: 'don't hire him.' "

The couple would also pay a lawyer to look over the contract. "Don't ask a lawyer friend or relative to peruse it for you as a favor," they advise. "It will probably get only a cursory look and you'll spend the money—and more—anyway when you hire another lawyer to untangle the mess."

Other advice from this sadder but wiser couple: if your instincts tell you things aren't right—even on Day One—listen. Better to pull out early and fight over, say, $20,000 than ignore the negligence until you're fighting over $200,000. Also, don't move out of your house until you must. And even then, visit the job site often. Don't make it easy for an overextended contractor to head out for other jobs—or not even show up in the first place.

contracts

You have the right to a specific and binding contract. The more details and pages it has, the better. Get specifics on every part of the project and on every product purchased. It is the details that will save you in the long run. Every contract should include basic items, such as:

- The contractor's name and proper company name, as listed on the business license
- The company's address, telephone, and fax number
- The company's business license number if applicable (Some states don't require licensing, but if your state does, find out the company's business license and verify it.)
- Details of what the contractor will and will not do during the project, such as daily cleanup around the site, final cleanup, security measures to be taken during the demolition phase, and so on
- A detailed list of all materials and products to be used, including the size, color, model, and brand name of every specific product (If you have written specifications, you'll need two signatures to change them— yours and the contractor's.)

- The approximate start date and substantial completion dates during the project (You might ask for estimated completion dates for various stages; for example, one-third, halfway, and two-thirds through the process.)
- Your signature required on all plans before work begins (This prevents last-minute changes being made without your knowledge and prevents misunderstandings. This way you get a chance to look at the plans one last time before walls come down and cabinets and sinks are placed on the wrong side of the room. One drawback to this provision is that it could cause delays if you are out of town during the renovation or are slow to respond. You may want to provide an address where you can be reached by overnight carrier or designate someone to sign in your absence.)
- Notification of your Right of Recision
- Procedures for handling changes in the scope of the work during the course of the project (The procedures should state how change orders will be handled by the contractor. Change orders should require both your signature and the contractor's.)

- A listing and full description of warranties that cover materials and workmanship for the entire project (Warranties are normally in force for one year, and should be identified as either "full" or "limited." A full warranty covers the full repair or replacement of faulty products, or your money is returned. A limited warranty indicates that replacements and refunds are limited in some regard. Limited warranty restrictions should be spelled out.)
- A binding arbitration clause in case of a disagreement (Arbitration enables both parties to resolve disputes quickly and effectively without litigation.)
- A provision for contractor's statements and waivers of liens to be provided to you prior to final payment

Include anything else that needs to be spelled out clearly. Remember: if it isn't in writing, it does not exist legally.

Most importantly, before signing any contract, be sure that you understand all of the components. You have the right to ask questions and to demand explanations. Never, ever, sign an incomplete contract.

LEFT AND BELOW
Will your project
involve significant
structural alterations
such as these? (See
the finished result on
page 179.) If so, con-
sider hiring an archi-
tect, design-build firm,
or house designer.
Although working with
a professional will
increase your initial
costs, it can steer
you away from costly
mistakes, saving you
money in the long run.

buyer beware

N'ann Harp of Smart Consumer Services says experiences like Magda and Sam's are all too familiar. It's very common, she explains, for contractors who underbid the previous job (and are, therefore, in financial trouble) to be seeking a hefty deposit from a new job (yours). "It's a downward spiral of desperation that ends in disaster on someone's job," she says. "It's not intentional fraud but bad business management." Beware of contractors asking for quick or large deposits or down payments, she adds. Here is more helpful advice from Harp.

- **Don't Judge a Crew By Its Logo.** "A smartly dressed crew with logo shirts and business cards does make a professional-looking presentation—and speaks well of the contractor's intention to bring polish to the enterprise—but does not mean that he or she is actually running a successful business. Always ask, 'How long have you been in business?' Anything less than five years is a red flag. Most businesses, including contracting firms, fail in the first five years."
- **Check References.** "We have found that references are extremely impor-

tant. Ask for the last three completed jobs and for a job older than one year. Ask for e-mail addresses as well as phone numbers for previous customers.

"Homeowners need to ask lots of questions, not just, 'Would you hire this person again?' Take the time to delve into details of the project with the previous customer. The complaints we most often hear are about the project going over-time and over-budget and finishing details being left undone. So it's particularly important to ask about these issues. And try to ascertain that the people you're talking to aren't relatives of the contractor."

Commenting on the people who didn't return Magda and Sam's phone calls, she agrees that it's suspicious, "A yellow flag, at best."

Trade references are also important. Ask for three suppliers, and be very wary if you find that the contractor does cash-only business with any of them. "Consider that a big red flag," she says. "When we can't confirm a business history or credit reference, we also see a red flag."

- **Get a Contract Review.** Harp agrees that Magda and Sam should have

hired a lawyer to examine the contract. "A review is literally worth its weight in gold," she says. "There are so many common mistakes, oversights, gaping holes, and sneaky language in the typical remodeling contract that judges often have trouble untangling them. Unfortunately, homeowners are rarely willing to pay for a construction-oriented lawyer's review."

- **Tie Payments to Performance.** Break the job into many small, sequential parts and tie small payments to specific performance for those parts.
- **Make Final Payment Significant.** Harp cautions against throwing away your most potent negotiating tool by agreeing to a modest final payment. "Fifteen to 20 percent of the job total will hold the contractor's attention—five percent won't," she says.

Finally, forget what you've heard about final payment being due "on substantial completion." Pay when the punch list has been completed. Harp believes that homeowners are sadly mistaken to expect that a contractor will come back to finish small jobs on a project for which they have been totally paid.

"Next time," says Magda, "I would only hire someone who has worked for people I know personally and got a glowing recommendation. Not just okay—glowing."

Another tip: Be there whenever the building inspector visits the job site. The contractor told the owners that he had put in a lolly column specified by the architect, and that the building inspector had okayed it. By now suspicious of everything the contractor said, Magda called the inspector, who did not remember the column; he visited the site and asked the contractor to open the wall so that he could take a look. The column wasn't

there. This, says Magda, is typical of the dance she and her contractor did for many months.

So why didn't they fire him sooner? "When the delays and problems first started," Magda recalls, "I thought some of his excuses were plausible—he lost his crew to other jobs; he needed to wait for plans before he could continue; he couldn't start the addition until plans were approved by the building department.

"By then he had done some work, and we gave him a little more money, and we sank a little further into the rabbit hole.

By the time we did want to fire him, we knew it would take six months to find someone else. Then he refused to do more until we paid more. So we negotiated and paid him some more and sank deeper into the hole. Then we figured if we could just push him. Finally, we realized it would never change; then we fired him."

Although Magda is convinced that this contractor from hell is a sociopath, part of his problem was poor business practices (and perhaps a lack of ethics, too). It finally emerged that he had taken on too much work and overextended himself, going from job to job and not finishing anything. Inevitably, he got into trouble on a big job and wasn't able to pay his crew; they in turn were reluctant to keep showing up for Magda and Sam's job, slowing down the process even more.

"My chief regret is that we did not involve a lawyer sooner," says Magda. "We do not routinely live that way and were very reluctant to make things unfriendly and stiff and formal. But in hindsight, I see that it was bound to get ugly anyway; we should have taken legal action sooner."

ABOVE AND OPPOSITE
In addition to providing all-important storage, cabinets contribute to the overall look of a space, whether it's a kitchen, above, or a family room, opposite. And buying new cabinets doesn't have to break your remodeling budget. Shop showrooms and home centers for stock units, many of which offer almost as many styles, sizes, finishes, and details as the more expensive custom lines.

should you do it yourself?

- Do you enjoy physical work?
- Do you have the time to do the job? Will it matter if the project remains unfinished for a period of time? (When gauging the time it will take, you should probably double it.)
- Are you persistent? Will the project get finished?
- Do you have the necessary skills—and tools—to do the job, including the expertise to install appliances, cabinets, and other equipment?
- Will you need assistance? If so, do you have access to a skilled labor pool?
- Are you familiar with local building codes and permit requirements?

- Have you considered safety issues? Some jobs—electricity, plumbing, roofing—have serious consequences if they are performed incorrectly.
- Can you get the materials you'll need? Who will be your supplier?
- Are you hoping to save money by doing it yourself? Will you, in fact, save once you factor in the cost of materials, your time, tools or helpers you may have to pay for, and mistakes you may have to correct?
- What will you do if something goes wrong and you can't correct it? (Most contractors are wary about stepping in to save a botched DIY job.)

money matters

FINANCING   WHAT SHOULD YOU EXPECT?

In today's society, there seems to be a somewhat casual attitude toward remodeling a home. People give plenty of thought to the finished product and energetically imagine themselves cooking in their shiny new kitchen, luxuriating in the amenities of a revamped bath, or enjoying happy times in the family room they've added to the house. Unfortunately, people don't always expend as much energy on the stages that lead up to the remodeling.

In the previous chapter, you learned the importance of assessing the feasibility of the project, hiring competent professionals, and checking their credentials, all important safeguards to ensure a successful project. In this chapter, you'll learn how to be proactive about money—not only obtaining the best financing but also staying on top of the budget.

A raised ceiling, new wall of windows, and a stone fireplace breathe new life into an older family room.

Everyone has heard horror stories about remodelings that cost thousands upon thousands more than the homeowners had expected. Yes, you may very well spend a bit more than you expected, but you don't have to lose control of your money. And if you take certain simple but important steps in preparation, you won't have to lose control of your household or forfeit your peace of mind while you undergo the project.

financing

Once you have made a decision to remodel—and have gleaned a rough idea of the likely costs, as suggested in Chapter 1—it's time to think about financing the project. Some types of loans—and there are several—will suit your situation better than others.

Begin exploring your options at your local bank, inquiring about available loan types and how much money will be made available to you. Your banker may offer you good terms, but keep looking. You may find better interest rates, lower closing costs, and more-attractive tax advantages at other banks, credit unions, savings and loan associations, even mortgage companies, which typically offer a wide range of options.

For small projects—under $5,000—some people prefer to use cash, a choice that circumvents interest, finance charges, and tedious paperwork. Withdrawing some of your savings, for which you may earn $3\frac{1}{2}$ percent interest, for example, could be smarter than taking out a loan with a 10-percent or more interest rate. The downside? Cash payments are not tax deductible.

Loans and Credit

Charging the remodeling to your credit card might also be a hassle-free choice, but only if the amount is small and you can pay it off right away. If not, there are options.

■ **Home-Equity Loan.** Often called a second mortgage, this fixed-rate, fixed-term loan is based on the amount of equity in your house. Most lending institutions will loan you up to 80 percent of your home's value and you pay it back monthly, just as you do your mortgage.

RIGHT
Will your budget permit a total overhaul of a room? If not, rely on refinishing the flooring, applying a vibrant shade of paint, or changing the window treatment to make a big impact.

■ **Home-Equity Line of Credit.** Also based on the value of your house, this option allows you to use the money as you need it, as you do with a checking account. You pay interest, usually charged at a variable rate, only on the money you use. You need to be disciplined, though, and able to resist the temptation to use the money for a trip to France or some other luxury. The interest paid on money you borrow from an equity line of credit may be tax deductible, but ask your accountant to be sure.

■ **Refinancing.** This allows you to use the loan you take out to pay off your existing mortgage and apply the remainder to your makeover. Refinancing is a good choice if interest rates are lower than they were when you first financed your home.

■ **Home Improvement Loan.** This loan, for which you use your home as collateral, is tax deductible and readily available.

You pay it off in installments. A possible downside is a higher interest rate than some other loan types.

■ **Federal Housing Administration (FHA) Loan.** This option offers long payback periods, typically 15 years, thus making monthly payments very manageable. Ask your local bank or accountant whether you qualify for one.

BELOW
Instead of a costly addition, a sun space gave a New Jersey family all the room they needed for relaxing and entertaining year-round.

OPPOSITE
The owners of this entry hall created architectural interest by opening up the ceiling and adding a dramatic window.

Establishing a Budget—and Sticking to It

You have followed the advice in Chapter 1, so you already have a rough idea of what your remodeling might cost. If you are successful in obtaining financing for that amount, you have the beginnings of a budget. Here's a rule of thumb suggested by the National Association of the Remodeling Industry (NARI)—once you have figured out how much you can spend on your remodeling project, devote 80 percent of that figure to the project and stow away the remaining 20 percent to cover unexpected problems

Be prepared to stick to your budget, and be honest with the people you interview about what you can spend. Remodeling professionals are generally amenable to working within your guidelines, provided they know your budgetary boundaries from the outset. And they may offer valuable suggestions for economizing. If they are not amenable, beware. A designer or contractor may appropriately decline the project because he or she cannot do it within your budget; but it is decidedly inappropriate for anyone to urge you to spend more than your parameters allow.

Because you have done your homework, you can be confident that your rough estimate of probable remodeling costs is in the right ballpark. Even so, the gap between your figures and the bids you receive may be wider than you expected. Resist the temptation to overspend in order to close the gap. Instead, renew your vow to stick to the budget and look for ways to trim costs. For example, you might consider changing the scope of the project by building a smaller addition or scaling back on the size of the revamped kitchen. You could also take on some of the work yourself. Doing the painting, for example, could save hundreds, maybe thousands of dollars, depending on the size of the project. You can also save by handling some simple demolition chores or by doing end-of-the-day cleanup yourself.

OPPOSITE
Built-in cabinetry can be expensive if you go the custom route, but you can save a few dollars doing the finishing work, such as painting, yourself.

RIGHT
Rather than simply tacking on a dining room here, the architect designed a distinctive entry into it, beautifully blending old and new spaces.

Substituting more-affordable materials, appliances, or fixtures for high-end ones is another effective way to balance the budget—choose an ultra-deep soaking tub instead of an expensive whirlpool; bead-board paneling instead of custom wainscoting; a mid-priced range instead of a top-of-the-line model. If your heart is really set on a luxury appliance, go for it; but offset that expense by choosing, say, ceramic-tile or plastic-laminate kitchen counters instead of pricey granite. You may also achieve big savings by buying some items yourself, rather than paying the contractor to shop. Check out home centers, factory-direct firms, salvage yards, even classified ads and auctions.

Another way to stay on budget is to be available daily to promptly make necessary decisions and keep the job from falling behind schedule. Once the job is underway, keep changes to a minimum. Some change orders are inevitable, of course, especially in a house that's more than 20 years old—termite damage may be found, code violations or corroded plumbing pipes may be uncovered—but you can minimize them by sticking to your original plan as closely as possible. Not only do last-minute changes add to the cost of materials, they can also put the project behind schedule, further increasing costs.

Prevent overspending by being as clear as possible about the scope of your makeover, as well as the materials you want to use or the equipment you will install. For example, in a kitchen makeover, don't be vague. Discussions with your design professional or contractor may have changed some of your ideas, but you should know exactly where the project stands before day one of the remodel. Make an addendum to the contract if necessary, but do not let any demolition or construction take place that is not part of your plan. For further cost-control, look over everything that is brought in before it's installed—is the lumber the size you specified; is the refrigerator the model you wanted; are the windows the ones you ordered? (Ideally, these items will be specified in the contract.) Do research on appliances, plumbing fixtures, flooring, and countertop materials. Find out to your own satisfaction which brands and types are right for you.

what should you expect?

Most of the projects covered in this book are fairly major ones and have the potential to disrupt your household, your peace of mind, and your budget. Don't worry, these are not the usual consequences of a makeover but could happen if you are not an educated consumer. As part of your preparation for the project, educate yourself about what to expect. If you are not clear about how the job should proceed, who does what, and when they do it, all sorts of things could happen—unnecessary upset, problems with the contractor, over-spending, and, worst of all, a makeover that ultimately does not suit your needs or satisfy your expectations.

staying organized

Your remodeling will run smoothly, says the National Association of the Remodeling Industry (NARI), if you keep the following documents in a safe and easily accessible location:

- Construction specs
- Your contract
- Construction schedule
- Pre-construction agreement
- Change orders
- Cost estimates
- Your budget
- Lien releases
- Construction drawings and plans
- Correspondence between you and your contractor
- Other correspondence or agreements with third-party participants
- Your idea book
- Paint chips, manufacturer samples, product literature
- A reduced copy of your plan to take along when shopping for materials, products, or appliances
- A list of questions to ask the architect or contractor
- Notes and reminders to yourself

LEFT
Don't rely solely on your designer to choose materials or a style for your project. Here, the homeowner explained her desire for large windows that reveal the garden.

ABOVE
To make this new breakfast room bright and airy, the homeowner chose tall casement windows, which coordinate with the home's architecture.

smart steps
be prepared

◼ Step 1 ANTICIPATE DELAYS

Your architect, designer, or contractor will give you a rough estimate for how long the project will take to complete. But expect the unexpected—the weather may interfere; materials may not arrive on time; especially in an older house, problems may be found that must be corrected before construction can proceed.

Delays will be stressful, but less so if you communicate daily with your architect or contractor. Many experts recommend keeping the project on track by holding weekly meetings with your contractor and, if possible, plumbers, electricians, or other major subcontractors working on the job that week. Attend these meetings even if you have hired an architect or a design/build firm to supervise the job. End-of-the-week meetings are most effective; but whenever you hold them, review the previous week, identify tasks that didn't get done, and talk about what is coming up in the new week, such as deliveries of materials and supplies or specific tasks like drywall or cabinet installation. The idea is to nip delays and other problems in the bud and to make sure everyone is on the same page of the project schedule, which you should have with you at these meetings.

Experts agree that one cause of delays is lack of coordination. What any job needs, he says, is a logical flow that assures foundations will be prepared for framers to build and framing is in place for drywallers

to install the material. If this sequence doesn't flow smoothly, grid-lock happens. And if the electrician disappears before the rough wiring is completed, the contractor may not be able to set up an inspection. This single delay could throw off the job by creating delays for carpenters, drywallers, and painters.

With so many tradespeople working on one job, schedules are bound to change. But weekly meetings will keep you on top of these changes and enable you and your contractor to find efficient and creative ways to work around them.

smart tip
SAVE THE LANDSCAPE

Don't let the remodeling crew loose in your garden without setting some boundaries. Show the contractor where it's safe to walk; point out prized plantings, or move them temporarily. Ask the crew to stack lumber on paved surfaces, not on the lawn. After construction, give your lawn a deep watering to help it recover from trampling.

ABOVE
Although these rooms have been updated for contemporary living, original details, such as the old wooden door frame saved by the homeowner, link them to their architectural past.

OPPOSITE
Before the project gets underway, talk to your contractor about ways to protect outdoor amenities, plants, and shrubs from construction debris and foot traffic.

■ Step 2 ANTICIPATE HOW IT WILL AFFECT YOUR HOUSEHOLD

Before day one of the makeover, schedule a family conference to talk about what is likely to happen. Acknowledge that the remodeling will disrupt normal family life, and make definite plans to offset the trauma. If your whole house will be disturbed, arrange to stay somewhere else for the duration. If only part of your house will be under siege, set up a room that is as far removed from the noise and dust as possible for family activies such as eating, reading, and watching TV.

You will probably have to empty one or more rooms of furniture, lamps, books, and so forth, and cram these items into other rooms, which will temporarily alter the peaceful flow of your household. Put away for safekeeping all valuable objects, and remove fragile items from walls and shelves, even in the rooms that adjoin the construction site.

The demolition and carpentry stages of the project will produce dust and grime. To combat this, cover your furniture in tarpaulins or old bed sheets and try to seal doorways with rolled-up towels or sheets of plastic; even so, be prepared for the reality that some of the fine dust will infiltrate. Cover the floors of rooms through which workers pass with drop cloths.

Kitchen makeovers pose a separate set of challenges. Without your usual food-preparation facilities, you may rely on eating out or bringing in take-out meals, fun for a while but ultimately tedious and expensive. Think about setting up cooking quarters in a room that's close to a source of running water and safely away from the work site. Efficiently equipped with a coffeemaker, small fridge or cooler, microwave, and toaster oven, this temporary kitchen can produce some simple homemade meals and help create a feeling of normalcy amidst construction chaos.

smart tip GROUND RULES

Set some rules in writing at the beginning. For example, designate a start time. Crews often begin work at 7 AM. If this will be a problem for you, ask for an 8 AM start time. Be clear about which areas of your house are off-limits to workers. Also, if loud music bothers you—or your neighbors—tell the contractor to control the noise level.

OPPOSITE
Updating an old house without compromising its period charm may require the expertise of an architect or interior designer.

BELOW
If you want to restore vintage features, look for materials such as antique doors or hardware at salvage yards.

RIGHT
Don't overlook new technology. For example, this engineered-wood floor comes pre-finished, which means no drying time.

The outside of your house will also be invaded by workers, equipment, and truckloads of lumber. Make preparations to keep trees, shrubs, and flowers safe. You may have to sacrifice some, but you can probably move most of them to a safe place temporarily. Request that workers stay out of your prized flowerbeds. If there are areas of your home that you wish to designate off limits to contractor and crew, make this clear before work starts. If those areas include the bathroom, ask the contractor to provide a portable toilet. Think about safety, too. Work zones should be strictly off-limits for children and pets.

Step 3 STAY AHEAD OF THE CHAOS

Experts at NARI suggest that you stay organized during the project by setting aside a convenient and safe place for all of your remodeling-related paperwork. For the duration of the project you will be receiving documents of different kinds—messages, schedules, invoices, change orders, and more. You'll need to refer to these documents from time to time, so it's important that you stow them in one organized and easy to find place. In addition, establish a communication area that will function as a day-to-day message center for you and your contractor.

scams and con men

Most contractors are fundamentally honest and hard-working. But beware of con artists. Some will take your money and run without doing any work. Others will take your money, do a slipshod job (such as "paving" a driveway with used motor oil), and *then* run. If you come across any of the following schemes or propositions, you should do the running:

- Door-to-door solicitation
- A one-time-only deal
- Someone who "just happens" to have materials leftover from another job in the neighborhood
- A request for cash only or full payment up front
- A pager or cell-phone number instead of a business telephone
- A post-office box instead of a street address
- Any kind of sales pressure, such as urging you to make up your mind quickly and sign a contract on the spot
- An out-of-state license plate

smart tip

SAVE THE LAWNMOWER

When you're remodeling, always look for stray nails and other debris on the lawn before they damage the lawn-mower. A foolproof way to do this is to drag an industrial bar magnet across the lawn a few times.

OPPOSITE

An attic renovation in an older house produced this charming bedroom. The cabinets are new, but the finish and hardware carry a patina of age that suits the room.

BELOW

Consider making outdoor living areas off-limits to contractor and crew. You may not want your patio used for lunch breaks.

3

kitchens

THE ROAD TO SUCCESS   EQUIPPING YOUR KITCHEN
CASE STUDIES: INTERVIEWS AND DESIGN WORKBOOKS

The kitchen is everyone's favorite room, even of homeowners who don't like to cook. It's the feel-good zone of the house, the place where people want to be whether they're cooking, eating, or just chatting. It's the room that's got to have it all—both down-home comfort and high style; sociability and efficiency; storage for everything; and room for two or more cooks, family, and friends. Because this convivial space contains many elements, it is one of the most complex rooms in the house to remodel. And its multipurpose nature also presents challenges. It must offer areas for work, adequate storage, and socializing. To coordinate all of this and come up with a good-looking room is no small task. Chapter 3 shows you how to approach it for success and gives you a glimpse into the minds and kitchens of people who have done it right.

To update today's kitchen the smart way, you'll need a careful plan that blends many elements into a cohesive whole.

ABOVE
ABOVE
Design cohesiveness counts. In this room, all the visual elements advance the cool, contemporary look that the owners wanted.

OPPOSITE
If a glamorous, efficient kitchen is your goal, think about hiring a professional even for a one-time-only consultation.

Working kitchens contain many elements—cabinets, appliances, flooring, countertops, and other surfaces. And the efficient functioning of a kitchen depends on several systems—electricity, plumbing, heating, cooling, and ventilation.

Because kitchen remodels are so complex, think twice before you decide to tackle the job yourself. To accomplish a successful makeover, your best bet may be to seek professional help. No, that's not to say you need therapy (although you may end up needing it if you try to manage a project like a kitchen remodel alone). Even if you have design and carpentry skills, it's wise to hire a professional—say, an architect, kitchen specialist, or interior designer—for a consultation. But whether or not you use a pro, follow these smart steps on your own.

smart steps
the road to success

Step 1 PLAN LIKE A PRO

Whether they are sumptuous or Spartan, big or little, the best kitchens have some essential features in common—they're right-sized, neither too large for efficiency nor too small for elbow room; they're easy to navigate; the work centers are conveniently close but not cramped; a logical storage scheme places most-used items at hand; surfaces are durable and easy to keep clean; and overall, the look is attractive and welcoming. Incorporating all of this into a functioning design that works for you sounds like a gargantuan task. It is a tall order but not impossible—all it takes is thought and planning.

Begin your approach as the kitchen professionals do—by first identifying what you and your family want and need. Hold a family "conference," and encourage everyone to participate. You might launch the discussion as follows, "If price weren't an object, what would your ideal kitchen contain?" The ideas will come fast and furious. You'll probably have to eliminate some of them, but others may become important items in your ideal kitchen, so get them all down on paper.

Take another cue from the pros and pinpoint the problems you are trying to solve. What do you like about the present kitchen? Conversely, what's wrong with it? Too small, too dark, hopelessly out of date,

isolated from activity areas? Is it so small that only an addition can solve the problem? If so, does your budget allow for one? Is it so hopeless that you must gut the room and start all over? Perhaps expanding space and performing a cosmetic update will do the trick. Look at adjacent areas—is there a hallway, closet, pantry, or part of another room you can convert into kitchen space?

C. Eileen Hess, CKD and ASID, a certified kitchen designer and interior designer in Westerville, Ohio, typically asks her clients to ponder some of the following questions. The answers, she says, make it clear how she can give them the function they need and the look they want. Nail down function first, Hess advises; the rest will follow.

■ How many people will be cooking at the same time? Is the current work zone too tight for two or more cooks?

■ Is your work zone efficient? Are counter space and storage capacity adequate? Do poor traffic patterns disrupt the flow? Do you have to take an excessive amount of steps during meal preparation?

■ What activities take place in addition to cooking and cleanup—homework, bill-paying, menu planning, entertaining? Do you entertain formally or casually? How many people will you entertain? Do you like the idea of people in the kitchen while you cook? Will you need space for a dining table and chairs?

■ Do you need to replace—or add—appliances? Will a second sink improve function?

■ Will you add any special features—an island or peninsula, a baking center, wine storage, bar area, recycling center, desk, computer, television set?

■ Is the lighting—natural and artificial—adequate? Are there enough electrical outlets?

■ Do any family members have physical limitations or special needs?

With the practicalities covered, Hess goes on to interview clients about style, quizzing them about the look they want and the cabinet styles, materials, and colors they prefer.

As you adapt these questions to your own needs, take your time with them—the answers will reveal what kind of kitchen suits your household and what you must do to achieve it.

RIGHT
A well-designed family kitchen may devote a corner to a planning area or message center complete with computer, telephone, and shelves for a cookbook collection.

OPPOSITE
A wine rack topped with a graceful carved arch becomes a design feature. Set on the far side of an island, it's close to the action but not in the way of the cook.

■ Step 2 CREATE A LOGICAL LAYOUT

Chances are, the biggest problem in your present kitchen is the layout. Maybe your needs have changed and the current arrangement doesn't work anymore. Maybe it never did work. Whatever the case, now's the time to fix it.

For your update, you can choose from five basic layouts, all of which are built around the hallowed work triangle. (See page 58.) One of the shapes is sure to suit the way you cook, clean up, and generally move around the room. The work triangle was developed in 1949 by the Building Research Council at the University of Illinois School of Architecture as a way to optimize efficiency in the residential kitchen. In each kitchen, researchers said, there are three identifiable work centers—refrigerator, cooktop, and sink. Each should occupy a point in the triangle, the total length of which should be no less than 15 feet and no more than 22 feet. Further, the researchers found that work zones, measured from their center points, were best situated at least 4 feet but no more than 9 feet apart. These dimensions ensure that work in one zone will not interfere with work at another zone. With less than 4 feet, collisions occurred; with more than 9 feet, the cook had to walk too far. And the triangle functioned best, they found, if no traffic passed through it.

Although not a hard-and-fast rule, the work triangle is a helpful tool for creating an efficient layout and can easily be adjusted for today's multifunctional, multiple-cook kitchens—allowing more than the standard 42 inches of width for each work area, for example.

LEFT
The dimensions are modest here, but strategic planning puts the work areas and storage cabinets within easy reach of the cook.

ABOVE
A U-shape layout is the most efficient. Add an island to the mix, and you extend both work space and storage capacity.

OPPOSITE
Closing one end to traffic in this sleek galley kitchen minimizes the possibility of gridlock in the work zone.

The five basic layouts—One-wall, Galley, L-shape, U-shape, and G-shape—are also helpful tools. Keep in mind that these shapes are suggestions, not hard and fast rules. Choose the one that best fits the space you have and the way you want to use it.

■ In the One-wall plan, work centers are arranged single file. Usually found in tiny city apartments, this is the least efficient shape because it provides no opportunity for a work triangle.

■ With two parallel rows of work space, the Galley, or Corridor, shape makes good use of a work triangle; and in a compact configuration such as this, moving between zones is as easy as turning around. There are drawbacks, however. A galley plan isn't suitable for more than one cook; and if both ends of the corridor are open, traffic will be a problem.

■ An L-shape plan places work areas on two perpendicular walls with one long and one short leg, and lends itself to an efficient work triangle without the problem of through traffic. Two cooks can work in this layout, and if space allows, an island can be added to beef up storage and counter area.

■ The U-shape, which many experts call the most efficient, arranges work centers along three walls with plenty of space for two work triangles for two cooks. The G-shape, an extended U with a fourth leg added in the form of peninsula, is also ideal for two cooks and offers abundant counter space.

When there is enough space, islands and peninsulas increase kitchen function, creating additional food-prep space, storage capabilities, or a mini eating area.

If your dream kitchen depends on an eating area, add a dining table (being sure to place it several steps away from the primary food-prep zone) or build in a banquette or booth.

OPPOSITE
Adding an island to a one-wall layout creates a corridor configuration, which is more functional. The multipurpose island serves as food-prep space, serving counter, or snack bar.

ONE-WALL
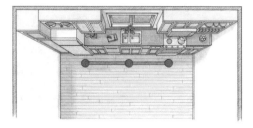

GALLEY
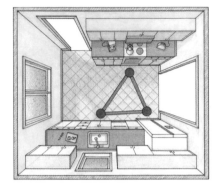

L-SHAPE
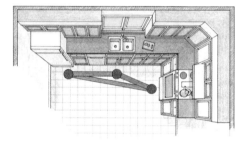

U-SHAPE
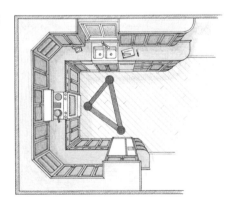

G-SHAPE
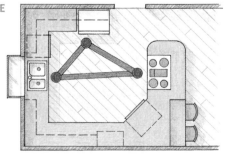

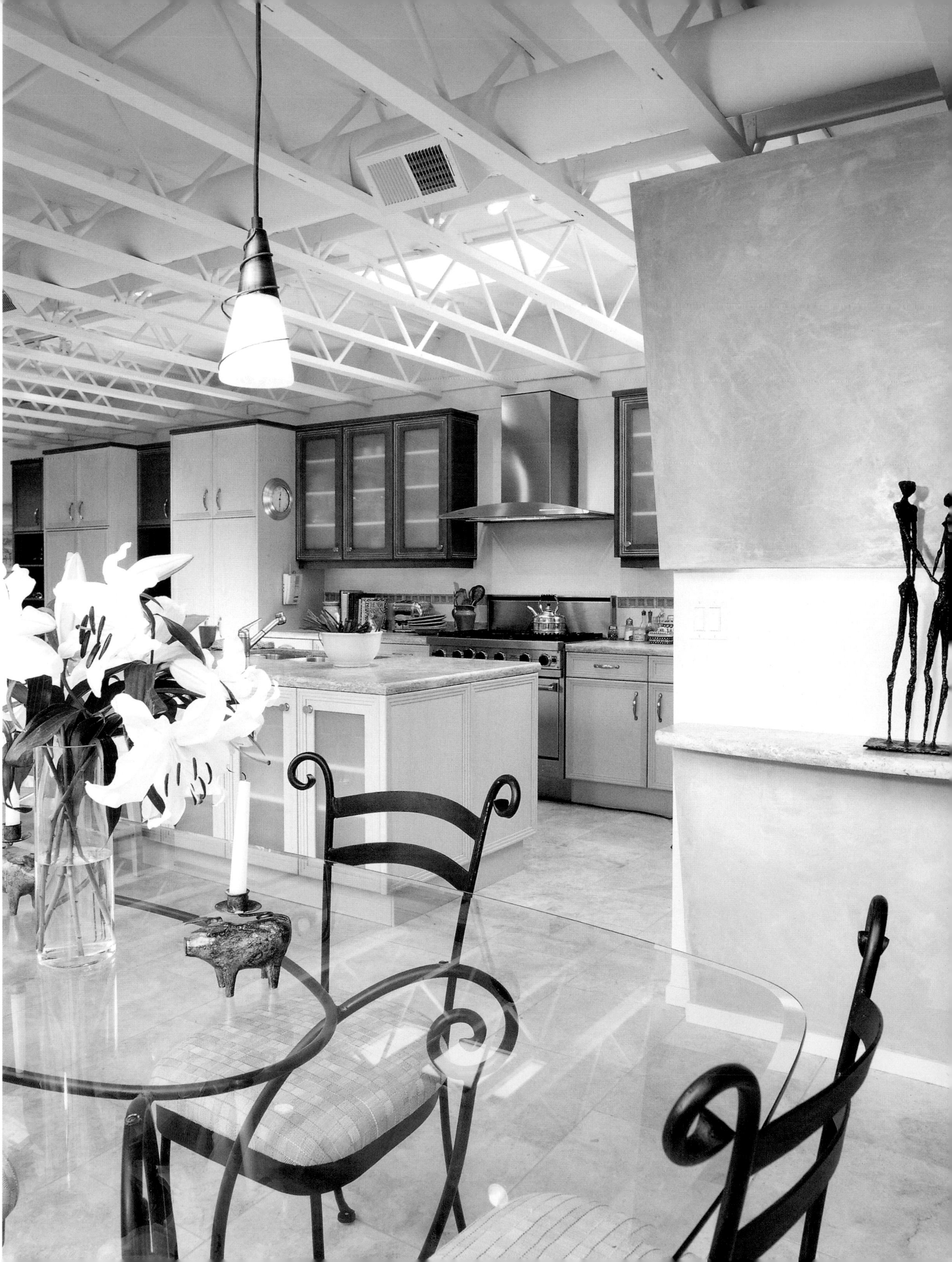

universal design

An approach that adapts the home environment to people of all ages and skills, universal design evolved as a response to a society that is living longer; incorporating it into your kitchen remodeling is a smart idea, particularly if you plan to stay in your house as you grow older. And including some universal-design features now will save you money in the future, when making changes will be more expensive.

- Install counters at varying heights, which allows you to do some work sitting and some standing but eliminates the need for bending
- Add a pullout counter near both the cooktop and the oven to provide handy landing places for hot pots
- Design an extra-compact work triangle to eliminate the need for extra steps
- Choose appliances with digital displays, which are easy to read
- Mount wall switches and outlets at the universal reach range—15 to 48 inches from the floor
- Select lever-style faucet handles
- Opt for a side-by-side refrigerator-freezer that makes both fresh and frozen foods easily accessible
- Equip cabinets with magnetic latches so that light pressure on the door will open the cabinet

OPPOSITE
Exposed beams and ducts overhead and a glass dining table surrounded by sculpturesque metal chairs magnify the design drama of this room.

TOP RIGHT
This is smart placement for a planning desk—close to the kitchen but out of the way of food preparation and cleanup. The little peninsula has rounded corners for safety.

RIGHT
Wide aisles make moving around this kitchen easy for everyone. Placing the range away from the main traffic aisle is an additional safety feature.

■ Step 3 SELECT A STYLE

This is the fun part of kitchen planning. Now that you have tackled the practical aspects of the room, you can get creative and select a style—or perhaps a mix of styles—that expresses your tastes and your personality. And in matters of style, anything goes, making this part of the process even more fun. Well, almost anything goes; the pros would advise you to choose a look that's in keeping with the rest of your house, especially with the rooms that adjoin your kitchen. With an open-plan kitchen-living-dining area, this design continuity is even more important.

Take a tip from the pros and select your style by looking through magazines, design books, and cabinet catalogs, or taking cues from kitchen showrooms, decorators' showhouses, even the rooms in your own home.

What rooms do you like best? Why? Collect samples of cabinet woods, paint, tile, wallpaper, and fabric, and live with them for a while. The colors, wood tones, cabinet details, and overall mood that you love best will soon emerge. Once they do, you're on your way.

If a slightly formal <u>traditional</u> look pleases you, choose cabinets with fine-furniture detailing done up in rich finishes such as cherry or mahogany or select white or ivory paint in a glossy finish. Enhance the style with natural or faux-stone countertops and wood or tile floors. This is an elegant, gracious look that draws on design elements from the past, so bring in glowing, deep colors, such as emerald green or burgundy; select floral fabrics for curtains or chair seats; add ornate moldings and a beveled or bull-nose edge treatment to the countertops.

FAR LEFT
Glass-fronted cabinets and a wood floor create a warm, traditional look even in a tall space like this one.

LEFT
Placed between the kitchen and adjoining living space, a peninsula defines space and acts as an informal eating area.

ABOVE
In a rustic vacation cabin, richly grained oak cabinets and granite counters strike an appropriately casual note.

equipping your kitchen

Has it been a while since your last kitchen upgrade? If so, your cabinets have seen better days, your appliances are dated, and your floors and countertops are looking a little shabby. You'll want to bring it all up to speed, but be cautious. There is more equipment in the kitchen than in any other room in your home, and you can spend a fortune updating it. And even if your budget allows it, why buy something that's fancier or more expensive than you really need or replace items that are actually adequate? Shop smart, and save your money for something you really do care about.

ABOVE
The designer of this period kitchen banished disruptive signs of modern technology by covering the doors of the integrated refrigerator and freezer drawers with panels custom-made to match the cabinets.

LEFT
Here's a bonus for a baker: in a specialized section of a kitchen, a mixer pops up to counter height when the cabinet door opens; a shelf underneath holds essential ingredients.

OPPOSITE
If you've got the space, put in a pantry next to the main kitchen. This one stores the "good" china and glassware and also functions as a bar.

OPPOSITE FAR RIGHT
Wine aficionados will appreciate an eye-level storage unit for their prized collection in a built-in wine cooler. Dark-stained cabinets reveal Old World details.

Cabinets

More than any other element, cabinets determine the character of the room and set the stage for its decor. Become familiar with the kinds and styles of cabinets available by checking out showrooms, magazines, and manufacturers' web sites and catalogs—and get cost estimates whenever possible. The cost of the cabinets you like plus a rough idea of the number of units you'll need will equal a ballpark figure for the cabinet portion of your revamped kitchen, which according to experts is about 40 percent of the total.

Here's a foolproof way to figure how many cabinets you'll need—empty the contents of your present ones, and combine everything you want to store. Each pile of dishes, glasses, pots and pans, cookie sheets, roasting pans, mixing bowl, flatware, and so on represents one, or maybe more than one, of the cupboards you now require. If this method proves too disruptive or time-consuming, study your present storage situation and estimate your needs, allowing for items that you will accumulate over time. Or you could rely on recent research by the National Kitchen & Bath Association (NKBA), which indicates that most kitchens require enough cabinets to store 800 separate items.

Cabinets run the gamut from very inexpensive to shockingly pricey. You can save money with knockdown units that you assemble yourself, but check them carefully—the quality is not always good. Mass-produced stock cabinets, issued only in standard sizes and limited styles and finishes, are also an economical choice if quality is good. Semi-custom cabinets are limited to standard sizes, too, but many styles, finishes, interior options, and accessories are offered. Custom cabinets, as the name suggests, are built to your specifications. You'll pay a premium price, but you'll get a one-of-a-kind kitchen with a personalized look and made-to-order storage.

The style you like best, or something very close to it, will be available in all of these price ranges. If the price of new cabinets threatens to break your budget, think about giving your kitchen a fresh look by painting or staining the doors of your current ones or simply adding new hardware.

Whether you choose stock or custom, frame or frameless, scrutinize cabinet construction before you buy. Look for sturdy cases, finished interiors, adjustable shelves, and solidly attached hinges. Look, too, for well-built drawers—avoid ones that are merely glued or stapled together.

Appliances and Fixtures

If you haven't kept up with developments, the variety of today's appliances will amaze you. Advancements include equipment that you can customize to suit your cooking style; faster cooking times; ranges that save energy, mix cooking fuels, and "think" for you; and refrigerators that offer separate temperature zones and handy configurations—including modules that can be placed anywhere in the kitchen.

The influence of restaurant-style equipment can be seen in the look of conventional ranges, ovens, and cooktops, and in their performance, particularly the ability to control heat precisely. For two-cook kitchens, *hubs,* or mini-cooking stations, can be custom-configured with one or two burners plus, say, a steamer, grill, or deep fryer.

These features can be wonderfully handy, depending on your needs, but your best strategy is to buy the highest quality that you can afford and don't let yourself be seduced by fancy features you won't really use.

LEFT
Bifold doors and cabinet drawer fronts disguise appliances. Customized modular refrigeration allows point-of-use convenience.

BELOW
Custom kitchen cabinets are built to your specifications and can accommodate special storage, such as this water-cooler cabinet.

OPPOSITE
Restaurant equipment remains an important kitchen trend. Before you buy, be sure your floor will support the appliance.

smart tip CUSTOM REFRIGERATION

In the old days, the refrigerator ruled. You put the bulky combination unit in a central place, if possible, then clustered your work zones around it to save steps. These days, thanks to the flexibility of modular cooling units that can be placed anywhere in the kitchen, you are no longer a slave to that one immovable behemoth, which is a special blessing for multiple-cook kitchens. You can provide point-of-use convenience in the bar area with a compact under-counter unit and an ice maker, or supply a secondary cooking station with a drawer-style refrigerator or freezer. Many combinations are possible—so get creative and customize. Integrated into the kitchen behind cabinet doors, you can't even tell they're there.

■ **Sinks and Faucets.** Plumbing fixtures have come a long way, too. Sinks come in bigger sizes, deeper bowls, new configurations, colors, and materials. Styles vary from farmhouse-style apron sinks to sleek stainless-steel models. You'll have no trouble finding a model, color, or material that matches your budget and enhances the decorating style you have chosen. But think about practicality first—if you have a dishwasher, a large single-bowl model may be sufficient; otherwise you'll need a double bowl with equal-size basins. For a two-cook kitchen, add a prep sink. A triple-bowl configuration with two basins for washing and rinsing and a third smaller basin is a good choice for a kitchen with no dishwasher and no space for a prep sink.

Today's faucets are so stylish and good-looking that you may be tempted to select one on the basis of glamour alone. But your best bet is to combine practicality and pizzazz. And beware of "bargain" faucets that use washers and plastic parts—they usually don't stand up to kitchen wear and tear. The best faucets are made of corrosion-resistant solid brass or a brass-based material and feature ball-style or ceramic-disk valves. Most cooks consider pullout spray heads a necessity; anti-scald features, swivel spouts, and water filters are also helpful.

Faucet finishes range from old standby chrome to bronze, brass, copper, nickel, colorful baked-on epoxies, and stainless steel. Most of these materials also come in satin or bushed finishes preferred by many homeowners because they don't show spots, smudges, or fingerprints.

LEFT
Hands down the most popular faucet these days, the pullout sprayer comes in a wide variety of materials and finishes.

OPPOSITE TOP
Here's a smart—and safe—storage idea: knives at the ready in slots custom-carved into a butcher-block food-prep counter.

OPPOSITE BOTTOM
Countertops have come a long way from the metal-trimmed laminates of the 1950s. Today's kitchen designers often create fancy edges using a mix of exotic materials.

smart tip INSTALLATION STYLES FOR FAUCETS

■ **CENTER-SET FITTINGS** require only one drilled hole. They combine a spout and two handles set in a single base about 4 in. apart, center to center. They are the least expensive installation type.

■ **WIDESPREAD FITTINGS** require three holes and appear to consist of three separate pieces. More costly than center-sets, these sets place hot and cold handles 8 to 12 in. apart, center to center, with the spout in between.

■ **SINGLE-HOLE FITTINGS** condense the spout and lever-style handle into one unit that provides both hot and cold water. Some come with an integrated spray setting.

■ **DECK-MOUNTED FAUCETS** are installed on the rim of the sink or into the counter around it.

■ **WALL-MOUNTED FAUCETS** are installed into the wall directly above the basin, or, in the case of pot-fillers, above the cooktop in the backsplash.

Materials

Whatever your budget or style preference, there is a countertop material to please you. The same can be said about flooring. However, people sometimes forget about flooring until the last minute, then make a hasty decision after they have selected the other elements.

Popular countertop choices include plastic laminate, ceramic tile, composite stone, natural stones such as granite, slate, and marble, and solid surfacing that looks like stone. Wood is a nice complement to a country decorating scheme; and concrete, stainless steel, and other metals are cutting-edge choices for contemporary-style rooms.

There are disadvantages to all of these materials—wood can warp or rot; solid surfacing and laminate scorch easily; ceramic tile is scorch-proof but can chip; the natural stones require periodic sealing. Some materials, such as laminates, are inexpensive; others—namely granite and marble—are costly;

most fall somewhere in between. Make your choice based on how much durability you need, how much you want to spend, how much maintenance you're willing to do, and what sort of look you're seeking.

When it comes to selecting your flooring material, do so early in the process, thus ensuring that it will harmonize with cabinets and counters. But it's not all about visual harmony. If the floor you select is durable and easy to maintain, you'll spend less time cleaning and more time enjoying your new kitchen.

Your choices are wide. Wood provides a warm look that suits any kitchen style, while minimalist materials, such as concrete and some natural stones, complement a contemporary look best. Marble and granite are beautiful and long lasting but can be slippery, and most natural stones need to be sealed periodically against stains. Sheet vinyl and laminate flooring, while not as durable as stone or wood, are cost effective and easy to clean.

When you shop, ask about maintenance. Some materials require more attention than others. How much cleaning do you want to do? Think about comfort, too. Some materials—wood, vinyl, laminate—"give" better than natural stone and ceramic tile. If you'll be on your feet for many hours, that's an important consideration.

smart tip COUNTERTOP EDGE TREATMENTS

Select an edge treatment for your countertop that matches the kitchen's architectural style.

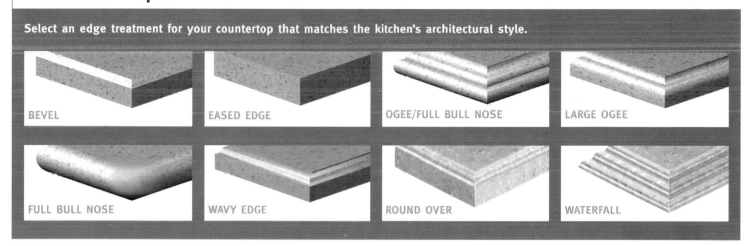

BEVEL | EASED EDGE | OGEE/FULL BULL NOSE | LARGE OGEE

FULL BULL NOSE | WAVY EDGE | ROUND OVER | WATERFALL

OPPOSITE TOP LEFT
Stone, both natural and synthetic, is an enduring kitchen trend.

OPPOSITE TOP RIGHT
Polished granite looks great on these counters but would be slippery underfoot.

OPPOSITE BOTTOM
Protect a wooden countertop from standing water, and devote some time to maintenance to keep it handsome for years.

RIGHT
Laminate flooring with the look of wood is an economical choice.

Lighting

Lighting is also often overlooked, but it is a very important kitchen element. Without it, the room won't be pleasant, efficient, or safe. If the phrase "lighting plan" sounds complicated or expensive, don't worry—it's not. Basically all you need to do is maximize natural light by adding new windows or enlarging existing ones and provide artificial light of two kinds—general illumination, usually accomplished with a couple of overhead fixtures, and task lighting, which zeroes in on food-prep areas. Any work you do in the kitchen—slicing, sautéing, rinsing, washing, reading recipes—requires at least 100 watts of incandescent (or 60 watts fluorescent) light. For countertop work areas, under-cabinet lighting is the most effective; and whether it takes the form of fluorescent strips, miniature track lights, or a low-voltage linear system, it should be installed close to the front edge of the cabinet so that it will bathe your counters in the kind of light you need for close work.

Under-cabinet strips or recessed downlights are often used to illuminate the sink; downlights are effective for lighting cooking areas, too, and some range hoods feature built-in lighting for the cooktop. If you will be using recessed ceiling fixtures or spots to illuminate a work counter, place them 2 feet away from the wall so that you aren't standing in your own shadow while you work.

ABOVE
Recessed lights brighten the cleanup zone, and pendants provide task light for the island.

RIGHT
A perfect choice for a traditional kitchen, the Palladian-style sink window brings in light and frames a garden view.

OPPOSITE
At night or on cloudy days, stylish hanging fixtures provide both ambient and task lighting.

“ My wife has the great ideas. I just

KITCHEN RENOVATION
case study

BEFORE

The Saratoga Springs, New York, center-hall Colonial that Mark and Lucianna Samu bought a couple of years ago was pleasant and roomy—3,500 square feet, in fact—but the kitchen posed some problems. "It was almost like an afterthought," says Mark. It measured a measly 200 square feet and was practically unusable because, as Mark recalls, "there was very little counter area; we had no place to put things down when we were cooking. And space was so tight that we had to stand to one side of the dishwasher in order to open it." Another drawback—the brown and white decor was bland and visually uninspiring, and it lacked the welcoming air that the couple wanted.

Without adding a single square foot, the Samus transformed this nightmarish room into a dream of a kitchen, as workable as it is good looking. Their first step—gut the old room completely. They then devised a layout that locates an efficient work zone in the center of the room and still allows space on the periphery for storage and a useful butler's pantry or mini-kitchen. A compact, two-tiered work island is used for most of the food prep; placed conveniently across from it is a cooktop with its own counter space and a cleanup center to the right. The haphazard old plan now has been reborn as a tight and workable triangle. But not too tight—there's still ample room to open dishwasher and cabinet doors.

Having laid out a logical plan, the couple then turned to the design and the details, with Lucianna doing most of the planning. "She's a genius," says Mark. "She comes up with the great ideas, and I do a little tweaking." One of Lucianna's great ideas was to place the cleanup area several feet from the wall and create a little

butler's pantry behind it. A handsome cabinet with diamond-paned glass doors covers the back wall and stores dishes, flatware, and table linens; across from it, tucked behind the cleanup counter's backsplash are a little fridge and a microwave. "It's very handy," says Mark. "The family room and dining room are both right across the hall, so people can come into this part of the kitchen, grab a soda, heat up a snack, or get what they need to set the dining table, all without getting in the way of the cook." A new door leads from this compact area out to the patio, where the family cooks, eats, and relaxes during warm weather.

Working with cabinetmaker Alex Stivala of Carpen House in Little Falls, New York, Lucianna Samu designed the cabinets, including the two decorative units that hold spices, dishes, and collectibles; the rest of the storage is consigned to base cabinets. "Lucianna doesn't like wall cabinets," Mark explains, "and I agree. They do seem to close in on you, especially in a relatively small space." To keep the room open and airy, she created a system of base units and deep drawers that hold the all of the kitchen essentials.

As they planned the logistics of the renovation, the couple gave thought also to the look they wanted. Warm and welcoming, a sort of "subdued" Country French, they decided. To create this ambiance, they selected cabinets with a traditional look, painted the wall a rich off-white, and came up with an eye-pleasing mix of materials—earthy concrete for the cleanup area, sleek stone for the cooktop counter, and mellow wood for the island and the two display cabinets. A jaunty fabric skirt under the sink provides a cheerful finishing touch.

AFTER

tweak them. "

design workbook
GREAT CABINETRY & MATERIALS

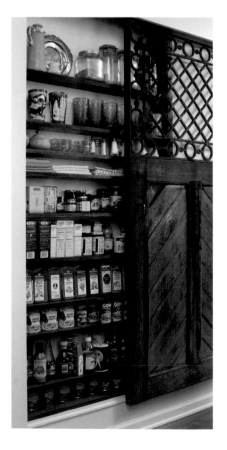

stylish storage

Glass-fronted display cabinets with the look of fine furniture combine with handsome base units to contain the clutter in the kitchen.

down to earth

Consider using trendy concrete for your countertops or even the sink. Properly sealed, it resists moisture and scratches. (See also top left.)

shallow but smart

Just right for small items, this shallow cabinet stores kitchen staples. The sliding door was salvaged from an old barn. (See also far left.)

easy does it

No more groping under the sink to find cleaning supplies. This storage drawer, left, slides all the way out, making contents easy to see and grab.

66 We call it modern Adirondack, warm

KITCHEN RENOVATION
case study

BEFORE

AFTER

The owners dreamed of an expansive kitchen where friends and family could gather, talk, drink some wine, and help the cook prepare the meal. When they bought their otherwise charming older house in upstate New York, they knew they couldn't get that dream kitchen without some structural alterations. The original kitchen had some serious flaws—first, it was too small to fulfill their dream; second, the layout did not lend itself to a comfortable gathering of people—or even to accommodating more than one cook; third, it lacked the character and warmth they were seeking.

Luckily, to correct problem number one, they did not have to build an addition, which would have been the most expensive and time-consuming route. Instead, working with interior designer and space planner Lucianna Samu, they looked around and discovered that they could add space by annexing the square footage of a couple of closets and a laundry room that adjoined the original kitchen. "By cutting out those areas, we were able to extend the kitchen by about 10 feet," says the husband.

A kitchen renovation this dramatic usually requires gutting the existing room, which the owners then proceeded to do, getting rid of old flooring, dilapidated cabinets, and past-their-prime appliances. They also removed the low ceiling and let the room soar up to the gabled roofline. Looking at the now-expansive room, the wife envisioned a huge island in the middle, acting as both a food-preparation surface and a center for socializing. Samu designed a massive 4 x 8-foot island that incorporates a sink, microwave, storage, and eating area complete with comfortable stools, and that is topped with durable natural stone, a work surface both functional and glamorous. Fearing that the island would look too massive in the center of the room, she specified that it be set on wheels. "Because it weighs a ton and is fitted with plumbing and electrical lines, it doesn't actually move," says the husband, "but the wheels definitely give it a lighter look."

Arranged in efficient mini-centers around the super-functional island are the work zones—a cooking area furnished with a pro-style range, a clean-up space, and a baking area with specialized storage for utensils and ingredients. But the pièce de résistance for the couple is the island, which welcomes friends, offers them a place to sit and work if they want to, yet separates them from the busy main food-prep place so that they never stray into the cooks' path. Guests can participate in meal preparation by washing greens or vegetables at the small sink set in the island, then chopping or assembling a salad at "their side" of the counter.

As befits a room in an older country house, the kitchen exudes warmth and charm, even though much of its equipment is cutting edge and current. "We call it 'modern Adirondack,' " they say. It's inviting and casual without being too countrified; it's up to date without looking cold or sterile.

During the day, light from two large windows brightens the room—a new window over the baking zone also ushers in some daylight. In the evenings or on overcast days, a well-planned lighting scheme provides overall illumination and task lighting focused on the busiest areas.

but up-to-date. "

design workbook
SMART SPACE PLANNING

masterful mix

The owners blended cool stone, rugged river rock, and warm woods, then added aluminum and stainless steel for sparkle.

cleanup's a breeze

A hard-working double-bowl sink, top left, is a good choice for a busy kitchen. A smaller island sink, near the range, provides extra support.

cook's delight

Upscale appliances and amenities include a built-in refrigerator and a microwave, plus a pot filler above the pro-style range, far left.

baker's corner

A stone countertop, left, doesn't get sticky when dough has been rolled out on it. Below-counter niches store rolling pins and other baking utensils.

4

baths

When you think about remodeling your bathroom, do you have visions of an expansive space with top-of-the-line fixtures, luxurious spa features, glamorous surfaces, and perhaps a panoramic view from the tub? That kind of room is certainly a possibility. But because the bathroom costs more per square foot to remodel than any other room in the house, you may have to adjust the fantasy a little. Like the kitchen, the bathroom consists of many elements—fixtures, fittings, storage, countertops, surfaces, safety features, and accessories, not to mention electricity, plumbing, lighting, heating, cooling, and ventilation. In this chapter, you'll learn how to approach your bathroom makeover the smart way so that you can correct its problems, meet your family's needs, and enjoy a few luxuries, all without breaking the budget.

The best bath makeovers include lots of light, room for grooming, and durable, easy-clean materials.

what do you need?

I t's hard to imagine that as recently as 40 years ago, a typical American house contained only one bath, and the whole family shared it. Today, we expect at least two, sometimes more, bathrooms in a newer house; and if we buy an older, one-bath home, we immediately try to find space for more. Architects and designers are reinforcing this trend, creating baths that accommodate the personalities, needs, and lifestyles of everyone in the household.

Whether you're planning to create a brand-new bath or remake an old one, the first step is to define your needs. What kind of bath does your household most need? An expansive master bath, a powder room? Maybe the guest room needs a little bath of its own or the family bath, used mostly by the kids, cries out for an upgrade.

■ **Master Bath.** Designed for one person or a couple, the master bath is often part of a suite of spaces that includes a bedroom, dressing area, closets, and perhaps even a sitting area. Some master baths, of course, are simpler than that; but simple or sumptuous, they all emphasize privacy and focus on amenities, such as soaking tubs, whirlpool baths, steam showers, or saunas, that provide relaxation from workaday tensions.

LEFT
Today's master baths focus on amenities that offer comfort such as a large soaking tub that's separate from the shower and a warming rack for towels.

RIGHT
Two sinks and a double vanity are highly desirable features in the master bath of a busy couple.

■ **Family Bath.** Unlike a master bath, which is used by only one or two people, family baths may have to service adults, children, and senior citizens in an extended family; and they require a plan that is flexible and convenient for everyone. If this is the only good-sized bath in your house, arrange it for privacy and multifunctional use. Reserve some of the space to create a private toilet compartment; place the tub and shower in one part of the room and the vanity in another, allowing one person to brush her teeth while another is showering.

To provide further privacy, install a small sink in the master bedroom—say, in a dressing area or in a corner of the room—to provide a place for shaving or applying makeup, leaving the main bath free for others.

■ **Kids' Bath.** A bath just for kids is a big bonus in a busy household. Use paint, wallpaper, even colorful fixtures to make it cheerful and bright so that it will appeal to little ones, but anticipate growing and changing needs, as well—the storage, grooming, and lighting requirements of an older child, for example. While kids are little, use sturdy stools so that they can reach counters. And equip the space with safety features.

BELOW
This family bath has it all—tub, double sinks, storage, and a laundry center. A whimsical bench helps little ones step up to the sink.

OPPOSITE
Here, cheerful color, an intriguing bowl-shaped lav, and a lower counter encourages kids to wash their hands and brush their teeth.

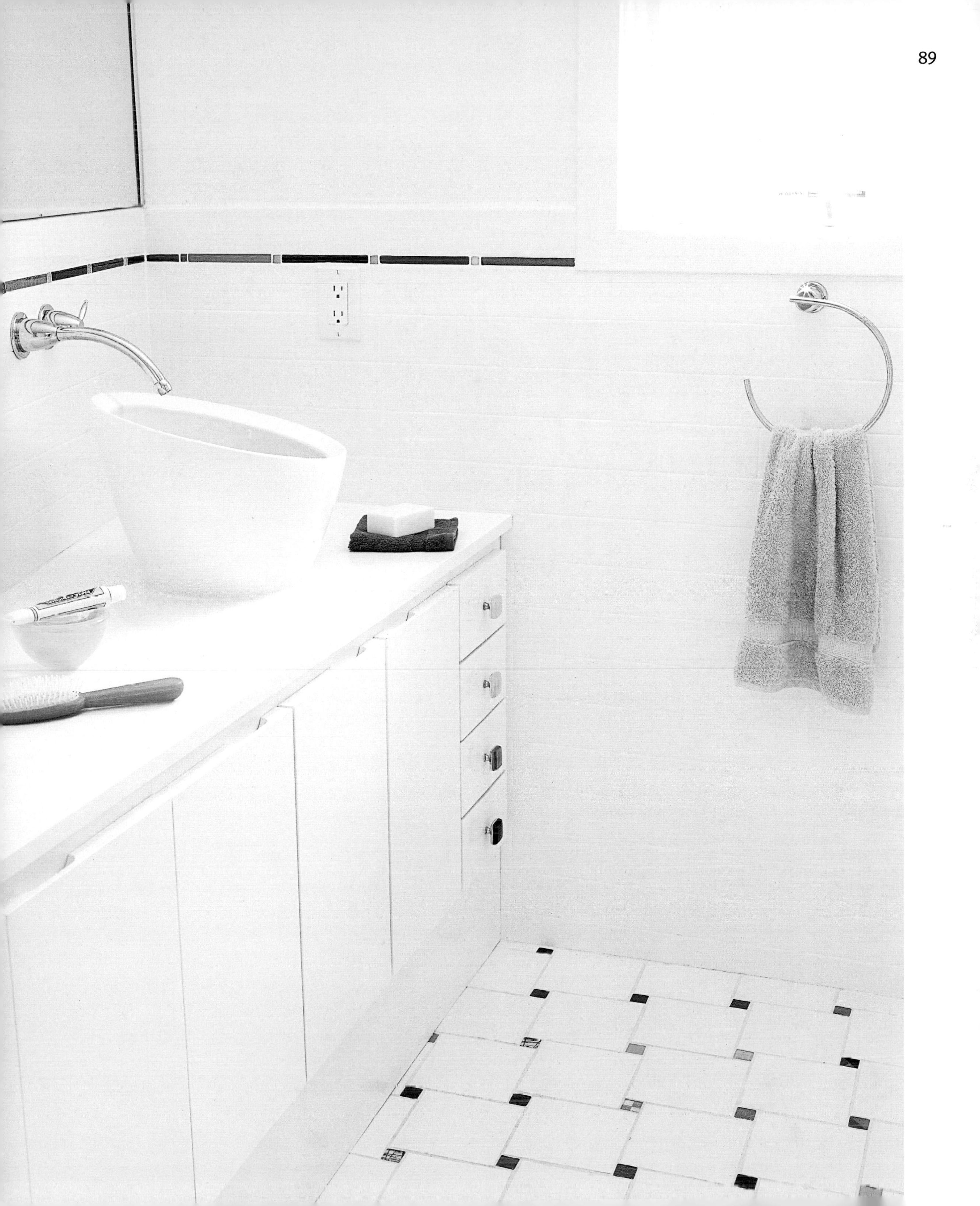

■ **Powder Rooms and Other Half-Baths.** Typically furnished with only a toilet and a sink, powder rooms are placed near activity areas of the household for the convenience of guests. If possible, locate this handy half-bath so that it does not open directly into a living, dining, or family room. Even a tiny space can serve as a powder room; to eliminate a cramped feeling, use small-scale fixtures and consider installing a pedestal sink, which takes up less floor space than a sink vanity. Include a mirror with lighting. Other likely places for a half-bath include near a guest room, in a finished basement, in a laundry room, or in the bedroom wing to supplement a family bath.

In most cases, remodeling a bath involves making use of space you already have. If you plan to build an addition, you can always include a bath in it; but to add a structure that contains only a bathroom is not practical. Bumping out the wall of an existing first-floor bath to add a few precious feet of space might be feasible; a bump-out that measures as little as 2 feet can add enough interior space to make a real difference and will not require a foundation. Other often-overlooked areas can yield bathroom square footage as well: closets, sections of hallway, or parts of bedrooms that share a wall with a bath can be converted into usable space. In older houses, possibilities such as this abound.

Another idea—if your house has one good-sized bath but the family needs two—is to divide the existing space into two smaller, side-by-side baths. You'll solve your problem and save money doing it because the rooms can share plumbing lines. Need a powder room? Parts of a hallway or unused space under a stairway are perfect candidates for conversion. The resulting room will be small but plenty big enough for a toilet and sink.

Rearranging an existing layout is another way to get a better bath. You'll be surprised to discover that a few minor changes in the floor plan can greatly improve the original layout.

RIGHT
Find space for a powder room under a stairway, as pictured, or in a seldom-used closet. To furnish it, all you really need is a toilet, sink, light fixture, and mirror.

OPPOSITE
Use visual tricks to make a small bath look bigger. Here, white tile walls and white fixtures reflect the natural light from two windows. The glass shower wall keeps the look airy.

The smart approach to a bath remodel is to put the layout first. True, it's the least glamorous aspect, but before you focus on good looks or exciting amenities, you'd better nail down the practicalities. A great bath has to be functional and well as beautiful.

Despite the fact that bathrooms have moved from utilitarian to luxurious, they are still comparatively small. And it is essential that they be planned so that there is plenty of room for each element. If you jam in too many amenities, the room will not be easy or pleasant to use or good to look at.

BELOW
To get the spacious bath they wanted, the homeowners annexed a little-used room next to the master bedroom, thereby creating enough space for a luxurious tub and a large walk-in shower.

OPPOSITE
Make sure the faucet set you purchase matches the lav. This widespread set, for example, requires a lav with three predrilled holes.

smart steps
create a layout

■ **Step 1** SKETCH THE OLD FLOOR PLAN

Begin with a rough sketch of the room as it is now, including any adjacent areas that might be used for expansion. Imitate the pros by transferring your sketch to graph paper with grids marked at $1/4$-inch intervals and a scale of $1/2$ inch equal to 1 foot. Your sketch doesn't have to be professionally drawn, but to be useful, it should accurately depict the space as it is now.

Measure the room—length and width. Record the measurement and position of windows and doors, including the swing of the doors. Note each dimension in feet and inches to the nearest $1/4$ inch. Draw in cabinets and plumbing fixtures and indicate their heights, lengths, and widths; measure the centerline of sinks, toilets, and bidets and record how far each of these fixtures is from the wall. Include symbols for light fixtures, electrical outlets, and heat registers.

While you're at it, list your gripes about the bathroom right on the sketch so that you can see at a glance what you want to change and what you want to keep.

■ **Step 2** MAKE TEMPLATES OF THE FIXTURES

With paper templates to move around on your plan you can experiment to your heart's content and eventually find a solution to your cramped, inefficient bathroom.

First draw the fixtures to scale on graph paper; then cut them out. As you position them, be sure to leave adequate space between fixtures. What looks okay on paper may not work in reality.

Step 3 PLACE THE FIXTURES

An efficient plan places the bathroom sink (which is used most often) closest to the door, followed by the toilet, then the tub or tub-shower unit, which are used less often. If there will be a separate tub and shower, place them near each other so that they can share plumbing lines. If space allows, place the toilet so it will not be visible when the door is open. Even in a small bath, the direction of the door swing can shield the toilet from view.

Another approach to placement—start with the largest fixtures first. If you have your heart set on a whirlpool tub and separate shower, pencil them in now.

After positioning the larger items, find a place for the lav—or lavs. Do you want two of them? Do you want them to sit next to each other or on opposite sides of the room? For side-by-side lavs, leave enough room for two people to maneuver; installing storage between them is one way to do this. Now position the toilet; if you will also install a bidet, position it, too, keeping in mind that you may also want this fixture out of sight when the door is open. With main items penciled in, start adding windows and doors and any extras you might yearn for, such as a sauna or supplemental storage. As you play with the design, keep practicalities in mind—plumbing lines, comfortable counter heights, safety features, and local codes. When planning the layout, try angling a sink or shower into a corner to free up some floor space. Consider installing a space-saving pocket door instead of a conventional one. You can also make a small bath feel roomier by bringing in natural light with a skylight or roof window or by replacing a small standard window with several units placed high on the wall for privacy.

LEFT
A smart choice for a small bath or powder room, a compact wall-hung corner sink like this marble model offers style and practicality without consuming precious floor space.

OPPOSITE
Think about setting aside space in your remodeled bath for a separate "toilet room," a real bonus for people who share a single bathroom. This one has etched-glass sliding doors and contains a bidet.

If you're doing a major update of your current bathroom, you may be replacing all of the fixtures and installing new cabinets and surfaces. In a less-exhaustive remodel, only a few fixtures will need to be replaced, and some fixtures can actually be successfully updated. A sturdy but discolored tub with a few chips or cracks, for example, can be refinished or relined; and shabby cabinets that are otherwise adequate can be refurbished with paint, stain, or new doors.

Before you go shopping, determine what needs replacing. Then select the bath products you need with practicality and ease of maintenance in mind, along with good looks.

Whatever the scope of your project, shop smart. Follow the same approach suggested for kitchen-product shopping—don't be seduced by glitzy, stylish equipment that will put you over-budget without actually meeting your needs. And remember that a high price does not always mean high quality. Find out what is different about a sink that costs $100, for example, and another that sells for much more. Then you can decide whether the higher price is worth it. A knowledgeable salesperson should be able to tell you; if not, contact the manufacturer. Many have toll-free numbers or Web sites set up to handle consumer questions.

Sometimes the reason for a price hike is a feature you can't see. For instance, a faucet with replaceable parts costs much more than a faucet with parts that cannot be replaced.

Compare each pricey product or feature with your real needs and your lifestyle. A sumptuous shower with 18 massaging hydrojets or a fancy whirlpool tub with spa-like features sounds luscious, but if your morning routine is a race against the clock to get to work on time, you may want to invest the money elsewhere— say, in an extra-deep tub that offers a relaxing soak at the end of the day at a fraction of the cost.

RIGHT
If your budget allows, splurge on a fancy feature, even a small one, that will give you pleasure. One idea is this cutting-edge above-counter vessel-style lav, which resembles an oval sculpture.

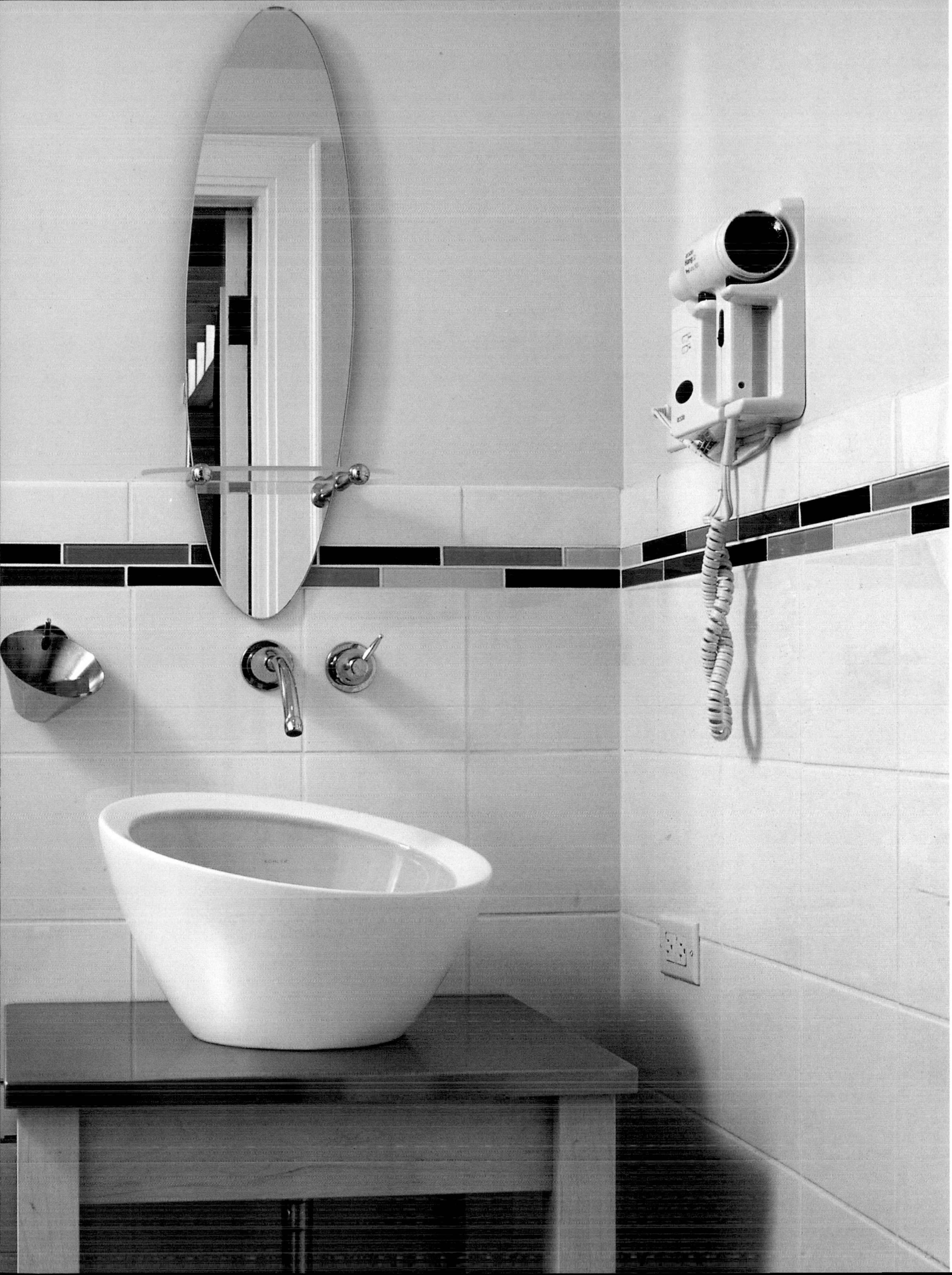

fixtures, fittings, and more

Tubs, showers, toilets, lavs, and faucets are the backbone of the bathroom, and all of them range from no-frills to fancy, economical to pricey. To guarantee a successful makeover, do your homework to discover which ones suit your space, needs, and budget.

Tubs, Showers, Toilets, and Lavs

With bathtubs, your choices vary from a standard unit with shower all the way to a large and luxurious whirlpool bubbling with water in a changing light show of soothing colors. Showers also cover a wide range—simple units to spa-like enclosures with fancy features such as multiple showerheads, body sprays, and even steam capabilities.

A basic two-piece toilet sells for about $100. One-piece models are more expensive, and if you add color, designer styling, or special features, the price goes way up. Another consideration is water conservation. Gone are a majority of the old 5-gallon-per-flush models, which were the largest daily user of household water. Now, according to a federal government mandate, toilets manufactured after January 1, 1992, must use no more than 1.6 gallons per flush. Manufacturers have met this challenge with water-saving gravity, pressure-assisted, and vacuum-flush models. A little research will indicate which model will best suit the needs of your household.

These days, lavs come in every price range and in many sizes, shapes, materials, and styles. Colored lavs are a bit pricier than white or ivory, as are hand-painted designs. If you will do anything at the sink besides washing your hands and face or brushing your teeth, consider choices in shape and size before you buy. A sink that is too shallow may not be suitable for washing hair or doing hand laundry; a handsome pedestal sink may not provide enough space for applying makeup, shaving or styling hair.

■ **Faucets.** When you buy a faucet, look for reliable washerless types with ceramic-disk valves and solid-brass or brass-and-metal innards; and make sure they fit the predrilled holes in your lav. Then look for the other features, styles, and finishes that suit your tastes and your budget. Among your choices are chrome, brass, bronze, nickel, copper, or even gold finishes; styles vary from old-fashioned to ultra-contemporary with many variations in between. If you don't want to spend time wiping water spots and smudges off your faucet, choose a satin finish instead of a polished one.

smart tip FAUCET LINGO

Want to be a savvy shopper? Buy a lav and faucet at the same time, matching them in style and making sure the fittings match the number of predrilled holes in the lav. Also, check that the faucet's spout reaches well into the basin.

■ **CENTER-SET FITTINGS require only one hole. They combine a spout and two handles that are set about 4 in. apart, center to center, in a single base.**
■ **WIDESPREAD FITTINGS require three predrilled holes. These faucets place hot- and cold-water controls 8 to 12 in. apart, center to center, with the spout generally in between them. Valves and spout appear to be separate.**
■ **SINGLE-HOLE FITTINGS require one hole and condense the spout and control for both hot and cold water into one unit.**

Any of these configurations can be DECK- or WALL-MOUNTED. Deck-mounted fittings are installed into the area surrounding the basin—the rim—or the countertop. Wall-mounted fittings are installed into the wall behind the basin. In either case, the spout must be long enough to direct water into the center of the bowl.

ABOVE
The owners chose a sleek, polished-brass, single-lever faucet to coordinate with other elements in this powder room. It takes up little room on the small stone-tile ledge that was created for the lav.

OPPOSITE
Glass, a trendy new bath material, sparkles here in a bowl-style lav. The faucet set—an extra-long spout and sleek cross-handle-style valves—has been mounted on the mirrored wall.

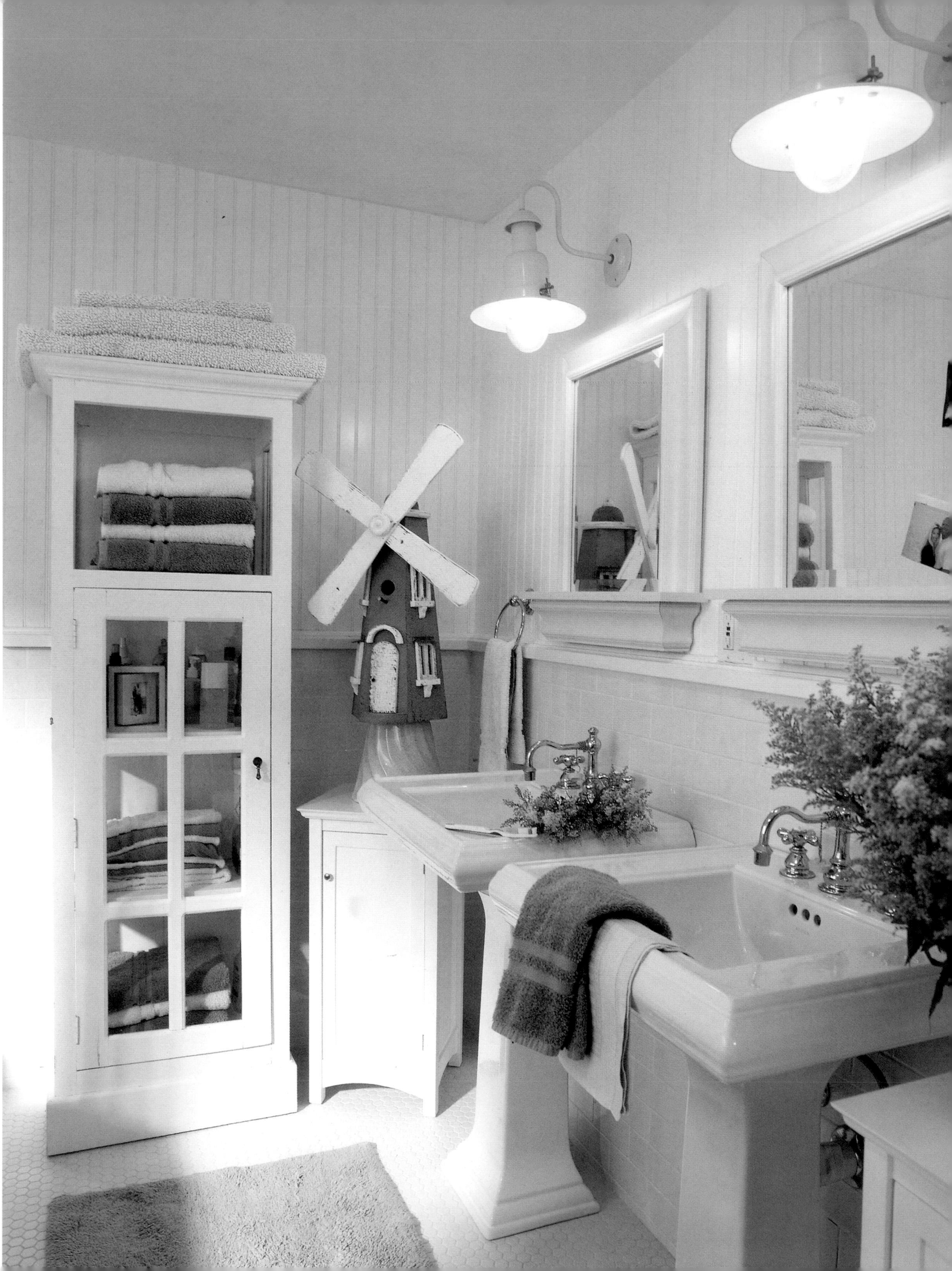

The Surfaces

Choose the materials for your bathroom for their good looks and easy maintenance. Because the bath's steamy, humid atmosphere can wreak havoc on walls, floors, and counters, durability and moisture resistance are also important considerations.

■ **Natural Materials.** Stone is durable, waterproof, and beautiful in any bath, whether traditional or contemporary; but if you plan to use it on the floor, select a honed or tumbled finish rather than a slippery smooth one. The same caution applies to ceramic tile, also long-lasting and less expensive than stone. Glazed, shiny tiles look good on counters or walls but are not safe underfoot; choose a gritty, nonslip finish for floors.

Wood walls, floors, or counters add richness and charm to the bath but need careful sealing to repel moisture or standing water. Concrete is highly fashionable today, especially for floors and countertops. Glass and metal are also cutting-edge choices for countertops.

■ **Synthetics.** Solid-surfacing material and composite stone come in a variety of colors and are nearly impervious to moisture and wear and tear. Although not as durable, plastic laminate offers more patterns, colors, and finishes than any other countertop material and is the most affordable. Laminate flooring is designed to look like wood, tile, or stone and provides easy-clean durability underfoot, as does resilient vinyl flooring, another economical choice.

OPPOSITE
White-on-white looks fresh and crisp. Ceramic tile and bead-board paneling are moderately priced materials.

BELOW
Today's large bathtubs are often encased in a platform of stone, concrete, engineered stone, tile, or wood panels.

lighting and ventilation

These two topics seem to be the least glamorous aspects of bath design, but they deserve as much attention as a pretty new sink or a steam shower. In fact, when properly addressed, lighting and ventilation can dramatically affect both your comfort and the appearance of your bath.

Ambient lighting, which typically comes from overhead fixtures or wall sconces, provides overall illumination and, equipped with dimming capabilities, can be lowered to make bath time soothing and serene. *Task lighting,* as its name implies, illuminates a particular area, usually the vanity, for close work such as shaving or applying makeup. Lights in the shower and over the tub are also useful and recommended to ensure safety.

Arrange your lighting scheme so that task and general illumination are provided by different switches; otherwise, with both types turned on at the same time, the lighting will be too bright and harsh.

For baths that measure 100 square feet or less, one overhead fixture is adequate; add another fixture for each 50 square feet of space. Supplement this with task lights around the grooming areas, over the tub, and in the shower.

Ventilation is a must to maintain healthy air quality and to combat the steam and condensation that can cause mold, mildew, and deterioration of surfaces. Your contractor, plumber, or electrician can help you choose the type of ventilating system that works best for your bath.

smart tip HOW MUCH LIGHT DO YOU NEED?

In all but the tiniest of bathrooms, ceiling-mounted lamps are necessary for sufficient general illumination. A good choice is recessed lighting. How much you need, of course, depends on the size of the room. If the bathroom is less than 100 sq. ft., one fixture is sufficient. Add another fixture for each additional 50 sq. ft. If the surfaces around the room are light-absorbing dark hues, such as mahogany-stained cabinets, deep-colored walls, or black granite countertops, you may have to compensate with stronger lamps. If the bulbs you are using do not provide enough general light, you need to substitute them with ones that have more lumens, not with higher-wattage bulbs. The next time you shop for bulbs, read the packaging, which indicates the lumens per watt (LPW) produced by a bulb.

OPPOSITE
During the day, diffused natural light is sufficient to illuminate bathing; at night, safety requires an overhead lighting fixture.

ABOVE
Part of your remodeling plan should include shadow-free task lighting at the bathroom mirror, where grooming takes place.

storage

The issue of storage is as crucial in the bath as it is in the kitchen, but it presents its own challenges. That gaping black hole under the vanity cabinet is clearly not enough to contain the linens, toiletries, medicines, and cleaning supplies that you will need to stow somewhere.

Whatever its size, a bathroom should contain a reasonable amount of storage. To get it, analyze the space and prioritize the items you must have handy, as well as any extras you'd like to store. Even a tiny 5 x 7-foot bath can accommodate spare rolls of toilet paper, additional bars of soap, a hair dryer, and a stack of clean towels, as long as you think storage issues through at the design stage of the project.

Bigger baths can accommodate cabinetry that provides a place for everything and looks stylish besides. But if your space is tight, you'll be happy to know that the tried-and-true vanity stores more today, and, of course, it can be supplemented by open shelves and narrow cabinets fitted into otherwise wasted spaces.

Like kitchen cabinets, units designed for the bath are available in many forms—knockdown, stock, semi-custom, and custom. Check out Chapter 3, "Kitchens," for suggestions on being a savvy cabinet shopper and getting the most for your money.

OPPOSITE
In "his" section of a master bath and dressing room, storage abounds, providing a place for every necessity and keeping counters clear for family photos and other personal items.

LEFT
Standing between his and her pedestal sinks, this handsome piece of bath furniture keeps toiletries and cosmetics handy for both users. Drawers in the base cabinet hold towels.

ABOVE
Natural stone and streamlined cabinets establish a crisp and classically modern look in this bath. The large vanity mirror visually expands space and reflects light from light-colored surfaces.

matters of style

Because the bath is now a "designer room," it has earned the right to look as beautiful and welcoming as the other rooms in your house. And if you select neutral fixtures—white, off-white, or beige—you can inject design pizzazz with details that are easy and economical to alter as trends change—wall paint, shower curtains, colorful towels, for example.

There is only one rule—please yourself. But chances are that your style preference falls into one of several categories—sleek contemporary, elegant traditional, casual country, or period-look Victorian.

If contemporary is your bag, you'll choose natural surfacing materials such as stone, glass, or metal; the frameless, streamlined cabinets will be made of wood, metal, or laminate; and colors will be neutral or bold. If privacy is an issue, cover the windows with tailored roman shades or fit the opening with glass block; otherwise, leave windows bare to reinforce the pared-down look.

Traditional baths emphasize richness in every detail. Wood cabinets in a mellow stain or glossy-white paint sport trimwork such as fluted panels or moldings; surfaces have the look of luxury—if marble, other types of stone, or ceramic tile are too pricey for your budget, faux-stone plastic laminates are an effective and economical substitute. A handsome antique (sealed against moisture if it's wood), brass fittings and hardware, and rich floral or striped curtains at the windows would pull this luxe look together nicely.

To establish a casual country style, start with simple wood cabinets stained a light maple; if the finish is crackled or distressed, so much the better. For the floor, choose wood (properly sealed, of course), wood-look laminate, ceramic tile or vinyl in an appropriate pattern. At the window, hang pretty curtains—white and lacy, striped, or gingham—and install fixtures and fittings with an old-fashioned look.

TOP
Although newly remodeled, this bath in an older house retains a traditional sensibility, especially the cabinets.

LEFT
Furniture-style vanities are an emerging trend. This imposing piece looks formal, as do the marble floor and wainscoting.

OPPOSITE
This space combines elements from many decorating styles—most notably country—to make a personal statement.

OPPOSITE
Period styles are perennially popular. Here, all of the elements—
some new, some antique—are faithful to the spirit of another time.

RIGHT
In this bath, a fanciful antique mirror takes the place of a conventional medicine cabinet. For safety's sake, bath specialists suggest
storing medicines somewhere other than the bathroom.

safety first

Thousands of accidents, some of them very serious, occur yearly in the bath. Here's how to keep yourself and your family safe:

- Use slip-resistant materials in wet areas—textured, matte-finished, or gritty surfaces for your floors and nonskid bottoms for bathmats.
- Install solidly anchored grab bars in each tub and shower. Towel holders and soap dishes cannot support enough weight to prevent a fall.
- Choose anti-scald faucets with easy-turn lever-style handles.
- Position tub and shower controls so that they are accessible from inside and outside the fixture.
- Make sure that glass, plastic, or any other breakable material is shatterproof, especially important in baths that kids use.
- Make your shower safer with shatterproof doors that open into the room and an entrance that's wide enough to negotiate comfortably.
- Protect electrical switches, outlets, and lighting fixtures with ground-fault circuit interrupters.
- Install a safety lock on the bathroom door, one that allows you to unlock the door from the outside.
- Don't keep medicines in the "medicine cabinet" unless it locks and is out of children's reach. Better still, store medicines and cleaning products somewhere away from the bathroom.
- Planning to sink your whirlpool tub into a platform? For safety's sake, maybe you should reconsider—the platform's steps can be slippery and hazardous.

“ The tub is 6 feet long, so you can

BATH RENOVATION
case study

BEFORE

AFTER

For the last several years, photographer Mark Samu and his wife, Lucianna, an interior designer and space planner, have been rescuing out-of-date houses, bringing them up to speed and selling or renting them. They began this profitable venture years ago in a carriage house they owned on Long Island. Honing their skills at special-effects painting, decorating, and simple home-improvement projects, they redid many rooms in that house. "Nobody is as good as Lucianna at making a house look great without spending a lot of money," says Mark

"Over the years our jobs have taken us into some multi-million-dollar houses and we've seen a lot of top-of-the-line design," he adds. "It stayed with us and inspired our renovations. The carriage house became a sort of showcase for our ideas; and when we moved upstate we started using those ideas in the run-down houses that we fix up. We love doing it, and most of the time we have a lot of fun. We stick to simple renovations and always work within existing space."

One of the houses the Samus adopted and improved—and lived in for a time—was a builders' center-hall colonial that was constructed in 1985. The house was a good size, but the individual rooms were small, and overall it lacked grace and efficiency. A case in point is the original master bath. It was an undersized and dated space without most of the amenities that people expect in a master bath today. It did, however, offer one useful feature—a long counter with two lavs and a large mirror hanging over it—but the couple felt that the pink plastic-laminate vanity countertop had to go. Even worse, the room was cramped; there was no bathtub; and the prefab, drop-in plastic shower was woefully inadequate.

Working within the existing space, the Samus gutted the room, laid a ceramic-tile floor, installed a bathtub, and replaced the Motel 6-type prefab shower with a sleek 4 x 5-foot walk-in enclosure lined in tile. The new extra-deep tub offers a luxurious soak and is a much more economical choice than a whirlpool. "The tub is 6 feet long, so you can really stretch out, and the water gets very high," says Mark. "It's great." They selected an acrylic model, mostly because a cast-iron one would have been very difficult to get up the stairs. Creamy-white walls and lush decorative touches complete the picture.

With the tub in place, there was no room for a vanity. Reluctant to tear down a wall, the Samus borrowed a 7 x 19-foot chunk of space from the adjoining master bedroom, enclosed it as a separate compartment, and equipped it with a vanity and a walk-in closet. The old hodgepodge bath is now an ideal master bath—efficient, private, and good-looking. And with the creation of this amenity-filled room, the house instantly became more appealing to potential buyers. (See the kitchen case study on page 77 in Chapter 3 for another of the Samus' home-renovation projects.)

Experience has taught this enterprising and creative couple about other value-enhancing home improvements. "Kitchens really sell a house," says Mark, "so do hardwood floors in any room. And lighting is more important than you would think. We install high hats, ceiling fixtures, sconces, and pendants whenever we can and hook them all up to dimmers. Potential buyers love all the possibilities." Another big plus—sturdy shelves in different sizes. Says Mark, "People like the idea that there will be enough storage, and they won't have to build it themselves."

really stretch out. "

design workbook
A MASTER-BATH SHOWCASE

surprisingly spacious

Separate but connected rooms for bathing and grooming make this remodeled master bathroom private and luxurious for its homeowners.

found object

The owners found this old sideboard at a yard sale. With plumbing and a stone countertop installed, it's become a great vanity. (See also top left.)

bathing beauty

A vintage-style pedestal tub offers a deep soak. (See also far left.) Molding frames a mirror that hangs vertically and opens up the space.

fit to be fabulous

The "French-telephone" tub fittings enrich the look of the bath, left, and feature a convenient hand-held sprayer. The walk-in shower is reflected in the mirror.

66 I added a little table to hold soaps,

AFTER

BATH RENOVATION
case study

BEFORE

Many people love the charm and period appeal of an older house; but once ensconced in it, they often discover that some amenities—such as a complete master suite—are lacking. Such was the case for owners of this bathroom. The second story of their 1920s Colonial house had plenty of bedrooms and two small baths, but none of these spaces could qualify as a master suite. Hoping to update this situation without having to build an addition, the homeowners called on interior designer Deidre Gatta of Artistic Designs by Deidre in Slingerlands, New York. To solve the problem, Gatta assessed the existing space, finally suggesting a reconfiguration that entailed tearing down a wall between two small bedrooms to make one large one and annexing part of a third bedroom to enlarge the original cramped 5 x 7-foot bathroom that is all too typical in houses of that era.

The old bath did contain all the basics—an alcove-style tub with a shower, toilet, and sink—but the fixtures and materials were ugly and dated, and the room was so crowded that it was almost unusable. After completely gutting the bath, Gatta rebuilt it, adding a bit more square footage but outfitting it with only a tub, shower, and toilet. To compartmentalize the bath and create privacy for the husband and wife users, she devoted part of the adjoining master bedroom to a grooming area with a luxurious vanity and two sinks.

In addition to meeting the practical needs of the owners, the remodeled bath adds glamour of a kind that is appropriate to the origins of the house. The claw-footed soaking tub, although new, exudes vintage charm, as does the marble wall tile. To add texture and visual interest, Gatta created a border of tiny gray slate tiles under the marble-tile chair rail. After covering the walls in a grayish-tan hue, part of a collection of historic paint colors, she decided to enliven it with hand-painted swirls in a custom color that matches the slate. She softened the lines of the swirls by gently rubbing them with cheesecloth while they were still a bit damp.

Another hand-painted item is a small table that is conveniently located next to the tub. "Because the vanity is on the other side of the bathroom wall, I added a little table to hold soaps, shampoos, sponges, towels, bath oil, and so forth," says Gatta. She faux-painted the top and edges to look like stone bordered by slate tiles.

If your idea of an interior designer is someone whose only expertise is fabric, furniture, and accessories, think again. Many designers do restrict their practices to such activities, but some, like Deidre Gatta, are also expert at enhancing the quality and function of interiors through space planning, nonload-bearing construction, lighting, selection of materials, and more. "You'll need an architect," Gatta says, "if you're putting in a foundation or adding new space, but if your goal is to make better use of space that already exists, an interior designer may be the right choice."

shampoos, sponges, towels..."

design workbook
AN INTERIOR DESIGNER'S TOUCH

decorative display

What could have been an ordinary little bath exudes extraordinary panache thanks to a collection of framed mirrors and prints. (See also top left.)

defining detail

Hand-painted swirls on the wall soften the geometric lines of the mirror frames and the slate tiles. They add a personal touch to the decor.

smart plumbing

Because there is no tub deck, and to keep the floor unobstructed, the elegant polished-brass fittings have been mounted on the wall.

shower power

The new walk-in shower, left, is sheathed in marble tile. The floor tiles are gray slate. Their small size provides a nonslip surface thanks to the many grout lines that add traction.

5

additions

Whatever its size, a successful addition improves the livability of your home. Perhaps it adds much needed living space, brings light into a murky interior, or exposes pleasant views that the original rooms had ignored. Some additions update older houses by adding living spaces that meet today's lifestyle needs. Additions may vary from small bump-outs to large attachments that can more than double the size of the original house. And if it's done right, an addition can improve the overall appearance of your home and beef up its market value.

It sounds promising. But this remodeling project may not be right for your house—or for you. For example, is your lot suitable for a bigger house? Will local codes allow you to build the kind of addition that you need? Or is moving to a new house a more economically feasible plan?

If your home needs more space, more natural light, or better views, an addition may be the solution.

In some cases, building the addition of your dreams may represent an over-improvement for your neighborhood, in which case you will not recover much of your investment at resale time. What's best for your situation? Here's how to figure it out.

preliminary
issues

Before you break ground for your addition, think it through carefully. A good place to start is with your local building authority. Why get all excited about your project only to discover that zoning ordinances and building codes in your community forbid additions or severely restrict the kind you can build? Regulations typically define the minimum lot size for each building and the maximum allowable size for a building on one of those lots; *setbacks* from the property lines delineate the area where you can build. Sometimes there's not much wiggle room.

Your local building authority can tell you what restrictions apply to your property. There may be height restrictions, design-preview requirements, or the need for a stamped architectural document or a survey. A local architect or contractor who knows how to deal effectively with the local building authority and planning board can help you weave your way through this process. While you're at it, you may want to commission a survey of your property, whether or not your city or town requires it. This document will identify where boundary lines and setbacks are located and where the house sits in relation to them, and it could become an important element in your planning process. Obtaining one early in the design phase is also helpful to architects and contractors.

There may be neighborhood limitations as well. Check your deed for *protective* or *restrictive* covenants that dictate the way additions should look and what parts of your house may or may not be altered; some of these covenants are quite specific.

Deed restrictions notwithstanding, you need to also give some thought to your neighbors. Do you enjoy good relationships with them? Are they resistant to change? Will they object to an addition? Will it impinge on them in a negative way—block their light, say, or obstruct their views? Talk to neighbors while you're still in the early stages of the project. If any of them voice legitimate complaints, you may be able to work out a compromise that's amenable to both of you—offering to plant some trees or shrubs, for instance, if your next-door neighbors fear that your addition will compromise their privacy.

smart tip EASEMENTS

Check your deed for easements on your land that restrict alterations. An easement may guarantee access to an adjacent property, or it could be a strip of your land that is used for a storm sewer, a telephone line, or some other utility.

OPPOSITE
Sun spaces are relatively economical additions, and they give
you a lot for your money, increasing usable living area, ushering
in natural light, and capturing views that the original house may
have overlooked.

RIGHT
Here's a bright idea for expanding and brightening your kitchen.
Add an abbreviated sun space—also called a bump-out—that will
extend floor space just enough to make a significant difference.

appealing your case

D on't despair if your proposed addition seems to conflict with a provision of the local zoning ordinance.
Depending on the conflict, you may be able to get permis-
sion anyway by appealing for a *variance* or exception.
Variances are typically granted if the petitioner will incur
hardship because the project is not allowed. If you sud-
denly face caring for an elderly parent, for example, you
may appeal for a variance to add an apartment onto your
house, even though apartments are not allowed in your
zone. An exception may be granted for a *permitted use* if
the project fits the intended spirit of the ordinance and
does not harm the interests of abutting property owners.
Ironically, *permitted use* in this case really means "permitted if you secure an exception." A home office might fall
in this category.

To appeal for an exception or variance, you will need
to apply in writing—usually on a form available at the
building department. The application may ask for a list
of names and addresses of each neighbor within a certain
distance from your property. You can get these from an
area map at the building, planning, or zoning department.
The municipality will then mail each of these neighbors a
copy of your request and inform them of the date of your
hearing. You'll also need a plot plan of your property,
drawn to scale, showing the existing house, property
lines, setbacks, and proposed addition.

You present your case at the hearing and hope that
any neighbors with a long-held grudge won't show up and
try to scuttle your project. It may help to get the support
of your neighbors well ahead of time and urge them to
show up to speak in favor of your appeal.

Does Adding On Make Sense?

Okay, so you are allowed to build an addition. But do you really need it? In most ways, adding on is more economical than building or moving to a new house, but why do it unnecessarily?

To answer this question you might convene a family discussion on the pros and cons of your existing space. Kick off this summit meeting by taking an inventory of the house and how well it meets each family member's needs. Begin with some basics: is the overall house large enough? Do specific rooms feel cramped? Do the placement of the building and the windows in it take advantage of pleasant views? Is there enough natural light?

Once you've gained some momentum with the initial questions, you'll easily move on to particulars. For example, you and your spouse both feel isolated in your small kitchen that's separate from the living space and would like to interact with family and guests when you're cooking; you'd also like a quiet place to unwind in the evening—kids' activities, music, and TV in the living room interfere with that. And maybe a sewing room would be nice, or an exercise space, or a place where plants could flourish in the sunlight. Soon the ideas are flying.

This rush of ideas may lay the groundwork for an addition, or it may lead to a realization that your problems can be solved by reorganizing existing space or improving current circulation patterns. Tearing down an interior wall could open the kitchen to an adjoining living area, thereby solving the isolation problem. To solve the noisy living-room challenge you might devote a corner of the master bedroom to a sitting area where you can retreat for quiet pursuits, or you may rearrange the dining room furniture to make space for a serene getaway with a small table, and lamp, and a couple of comfortable chairs. Just because your house seems cramped and dark doesn't mean it actually needs to be larger. Maybe you could solve that problem with a wall of windows or a set of French doors that open onto a new deck or patio. Any revamping of existing space would cost considerably less than adding on to it. There are other options.

RIGHT

Two-story additions are great space enhancers, but the design and placement of connecting stairs can be a challenge. Functioning as a major feature in a remodeled older house, this stairway smoothly links the levels of a large addition. Its architecturally classic detailing makes it look as though it's always been a part of the house.

BEFORE

■ **Bump It Out.** The simplest space expander of all, a bump-out requires no foundation. Instead, the outer wall of the room that is to be enlarged gets bumped out a few feet to hang off the house. The smallest bump-outs are available as mini-greenhouses that replace an existing window. These units allow more natural light into the space and make it feel larger without actually enlarging the room. But a bump-out that's only three or four feet deep may suffice to increase much needed counter space to a kitchen, expand a cramped dining area, or add a sunny sitting area to a master suite. Also, adding just a few usable square feet to a room can free up space in other parts of the house.

■ **Convert Existing Space.** Converting existing areas such as attics, basements, or garages can contribute new living space without the expense of excavating, building a foundation, and erecting new exterior walls.

AFTER

BELOW
To maximize natural light in this dining-room addition, the architect wrapped it in windows and topped it with two skylights.

However, it's best to have a design professional help you determine whether or not these areas can be successfully converted. Attic floors may need shoring up, for example; and dorm-

ers may be necessary to bring in light and air. Basements can be challenging, too—it may be difficult to make them watertight, create sufficient headroom, and bring in enough light. Attached garages, which often adjoin the kitchen, can become family rooms or even, with the addition of a bath, an extra bedroom or guest suite.

Porches, decks, carports, and other attached areas that already have a foundation and a structure that can act as a subfloor can also be converted into living space.

■ **Add a Sun Space.** Designed and positioned correctly, these spaces can capture light and heat from the sun, provide a cheery space to sit all winter, and make your houseplants very happy. If you choose a kit system you may get some design help from the manufacturer; if not, consult a specialist before you proceed. The angle of the sun, type of glazing, and choice of flooring materials are important issues in a sun space and should be reviewed by an expert. During the warmest months of the year, you may need air conditioning and special window treatments.

start with a plan

You will need some kind of plan of the property to help you conceive and build your addition. When you submit it to obtain a building permit, your site plan should include certain minimum data, such as the location of the house on the property, the property lines, the driveway, and aboveground and underground obstructions like utility lines. An arrow on the plan indicating true north won't be necessary, but it will help you in analyzing the effects of the climate on your addition.

This information must be drawn to scale (usually 1 inch = 20 feet, or larger). If you don't already have a site plan with this information, you can have one made by a surveyor, using the legal description on your deed as a starting point. The surveyor may need to take on-site measurements to verify the data or establish data not described in the deed.

If your site is very large, heavily sloped, wooded, or covered by ponds or streams, you might want a more detailed site plan that pegs the locations of these features and shows contours. A "topographical survey," such as this one (right), is made by a surveyor from raw data supplied by a crew at the site.

Site Plan

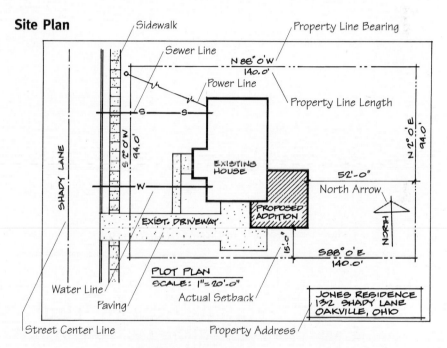

Contour Map

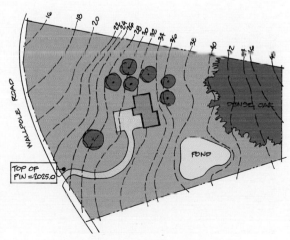

Can You Afford To Add On?

Next, determine the economic feasibility of an addition by considering these questions—is the money to build it available? Will it cost less than building or buying elsewhere? Will its finished value be equal to its cost or, better yet, even greater?

Because many homeowners move within a few years of making extensive home improvements, it makes sense to choose a project that will increase the market value of your house. A master suite, a family room, or a downstairs bath will very likely be attractive to potential home buyers. But any improvement that sets the house greatly apart from others on the block or is so quirky that it can't be converted to conventional use by the next owner may detract from the house's value.

If you intend to live in your house forever—and if other economic factors are favorable—go ahead and build the addition that suits your needs and enjoy it. But if resale is a possibility, think about payback potentials.

smart steps
do your homework

Step 1 STUDY YOUR NEIGHBORHOOD

What are houses selling for? What features do potential buyers expect—2½ baths, a master suite, an eat-in kitchen? What features are they likely to spend a bit extra to get?

The space you add will start paying you back immediately in the enhanced livability of your home. How much payback your improvement will yield on the money invested depends on the cost of the improvement and the market demand for this type of amenity when you sell your house. Predicting demand is risky, of course, but here are some general suggestions:

■ Try to price your remodeling project so that it keeps the overall value of your house steady somewhere between the low and high ends of the selling prices of nearby homes. Another way to look at this—keep your total remodeling budget within 15 to 20 percent of the value of your house before remodeling.

■ Don't fight the trend. You're more likely to recoup your investment if you plan your project for a time

BEFORE

LEFT, BELOW, AND OPPOSITE Some projects can make major improvements in your home's efficiency, livability, and resale value. When the homeowners built this family-room addition, they included a new fireplace—an amenity potential buyers desire today. Reclaimed bricks and a wood mantle salvaged from an old house give this one a vintage look that suits the house.

AFTER

when home values are generally rising in your area. One indication of a rising market is an increase in the number of other houses being improved.

■ When planning your project, remember that the more you customize a feature to suit your own needs, the less appealing it is likely to be to a potential buyer.

Step 2 CONSIDER THE PAYBACK POTENTIAL OF VARIOUS TYPES OF ADDITIONS

Some projects have greater potential than others for paying back some or all of your remodeling dollars at resale time.

■ Living or Family Rooms. If only one room is currently serving the household's social and leisure activities, an additional room will enhance your own enjoyment of your home and appeal to a potential buyer as well. To ensure the greatest return, plan the space for easy conversion to another use. For example, if you add a separate entrance to your new family room, it could become a home office for a future occupant.

■ Bathrooms. New bathroom space is expensive and won't necessarily add to the resale value of your house. If fact, if you have fewer baths than the other houses in your area, you may have to add one just to keep up. Conversely, if you add a fourth bath when the neighbors only have two, you probably won't recoup your money. The current demand is not for three or four baths but for amenities in one or two of them—if you add a bath, jazz it up a little with an extra-deep soaking tub, a whirlpool, or a separate shower with fancy features.

■ Kitchens. Everybody loves kitchens. The trouble is, everybody has pretty definite ideas about how a kitchen should look and function. It is very common for potential home buyers to look at a kitchen and immediately begin thinking about how they will alter it to their own needs and taste. The cost of the changes they want to make is what they factor into the price they're willing to pay, not the cost of the equipment or finishes that you have chosen and paid dearly for. Decide early in the planning process whether you want to spend money on your favorite features or whether you want to create a kitchen that will increase the resale value of your house. For instance a solid-surfacing countertop in your favorite color will cost many hundreds of dollars more than a plastic laminate counter in a neutral color. You won't recover the cost at resale time, but if that luscious and luxurious counter makes you happy, it may be worth it.

■ Home Offices. Dedicated at-home work spaces are popular at the moment, but there's no telling how long this trend may last. To get the most out of your investment, plan this space so that it can be easily converted to a bedroom by a future owner who may have no interest in working at home. An outside entrance will not be a drawback—in fact, it could appeal to a potential buyer—but draw the line at including items such as fluorescent overhead lights or built-in units, which lock the space into office use.

OPPOSITE AND ABOVE
If you're looking for big bucks from a dedicated home office at resale time, forget it: think about making do in the garage, as this charming example (opposite) illustrates. A new kitchen addition usually pays for most of Itself if you sell the house within a year or two.

types of additions

Building a *single-room addition* onto your property at the rear, side, or even front of your house is the most common—and easiest—way to expand actual space. A room addition needs a foundation, which is time-consuming and costly, but for the most part it is a straightforward kind of structure that is built out in the yard away from the living areas of the house, causing a minimum of disruption and confusion for the household. In most cases opening the room addition into the main house can be done at the end of the project, which further minimizes construction chaos. A two-story addition will cost more, of course, but it too is generally a straightforward project.

However, sometimes the only way to go is up. A *second-story addition* is an ideal way to expand a one-story house when yard space is at a premium or when neighboring houses stand so close that they block natural light, air, and views.

This type of addition is relatively easy and economical—provided that your house is structurally sound and can handle the load of a second story. Unfortunately, single-story houses, particularly newer ones, usually are not built to bear the weight of a second story, and in that case expensive structural alterations are required.

Other difficulties include removing the roof; finding a place for the interior connecting stairway without causing space or circulation problems on the first floor; and transporting building materials to the second level. Unlike a simple room addition, this type of construction does cause household disruption.

In some situations a *combination addition* is the best way to go. In this scenario, the new construction is built partly on ground level, as a simple room addition with two stories, and partly as a new second story, extending over a portion of the original house.

Generous enough to add significant space, compact enough to preserve the yard, and tall enough to capture light and views, this type of addition is especially attractive for a small lot. If the span is not overly long, the new first story offers some

BEFORE

OPPOSITE
Building up does not require a new foundation unless the new space needs additional structural support.

ABOVE AND RIGHT
By far the most economical way to increase living space is to use areas of your home that are already there—an attic, garage, or even basement are all potential candidates for conversion. This attic makeover provided a bedroom—and some extra privacy—for the owners' teenage daughter. Later, it can be used as a guest bedroom or a home office.

AFTER

ABOVE
Not sure how to blend your addition with existing space? An architect or interior designer can provide suggestions like these ceiling beams.

OPPOSITE
In this remodel, the owners enlarged their kitchen with a dining area and a deck. Extravagant use of white paint unifies inside and out.

structural support for the portion of the second story that cantilevers over the existing house. Stairs that connect the two stories cease to be a problem—because they can be built in the addition, they don't interfere with usable floor space.

Deciding which of these additions suits your spatial needs, your property, and the design and structural properties of your house is a complicated proposition. Even if you end up doing much of the work yourself, you'd be wise to consult an architect or structural engineer before you begin.

do you need professional help?

Chapter 1 described the design and remodeling professionals that a major project might require; it also talked about the possibility of doing the work yourself and saving a lot of money doing so. But before you commit yourself to a major undertaking such as planning and constructing an addi-

tion, take the quiz on page 31 of that chapter to see whether you meet most of the criteria—for example, do you own the necessary tools? Have you had experience with a similar project?

Keep in mind, too, that most additions need some preliminary excavation, a foundation, electricity, heating, cooling, and possibly plumbing. Unless you are skilled in all of these trades, you'll need to farm out some of the work. Do you have the time and ability to schedule the work, hire and coordinate subs, order materials, and do the required accounting? If you take on these responsibilities and later mismanage them, your potential savings will erode and the project could cost you more than you would have paid a general contractor in the first place.

But there's more to a successful addition than structural components, mechanical systems, and bookkeeping. You'll want it to harmonize with the exterior of your house and look at home on your property; inside, you'll want it to enhance livability and echo the aesthetic of existing spaces. To achieve all of this, you may need the assistance of an architect or other professional who has been trained to blend old and new exteriors, integrate new rooms into a workable overall plan, and establish effective traffic and circulation patterns.

ABOVE
In an effective juxtaposition of shapes, a round window and a rectangular skylight channel light into a kitchen addition.

RIGHT
To unify living space and a music room add-on, the designer repeated the flooring, window shapes, and moldings.

Experienced architects and designers use massing, scale, proportion, and materials to smoothly integrate a house and its addition. Pros also know how to place windows, doors, and other architectural elements to create rhythm and balance, gracefully punctuating, for example, a long wall with three well-placed windows rather than a single large window smack in the middle. Similarly, roofs of different sizes or heights with the same pitch and trim will unify old and new while creating more visual interest than a continuous roofline would.

An architect's or designer's fee will add to your budget, of course, but he or she may save you money in the long run by properly sizing the addition to your needs and your budget,

pointing out, for example, that a small amount of added space may solve your problems just as well as the large structure you had in mind. Also, a pro can tell you where best to locate an addition so that it will cause the least disruption to the site and take maximum advantage of natural light and outdoor vistas.

There are a couple of ways to work with an architect—hire one to oversee the entire project from beginning to end, or work on a consulting basis, with the architect producing a design, then leaving the rest of the project to you and your contractor.

Some other professionals with whom you might want to consider working—an interior designer, who can help you choose colors, furnishings, fabrics, and accessories that will blend the new space and with existing rooms; kitchen or bath designers, who can give you specialized help on these two complex rooms;

and landscape architects or garden designers, who specify the plantings and outdoor living areas that will link your addition to the existing house and its site.

If you don't do the construction yourself, you will also want to hire a contractor, who will handle all aspects of the construction from foundation to final details, overseeing any subcontractors you or he may hire. If there are contractors in your area who specialize in additions, you might want to consider working with one of them. Whoever you hire, be sure to follow the advice in Chapter 1—check references carefully, and develop an iron-clad contract.

blending old and new

A well-integrated addition will please the eye and increase the resale value of your house. And the reverse is also true—an addition that looks haphazard and hastily tacked-on can cause that resale value to plunge. Here are some tips for creating design harmony.

- **Rooflines.** To maintain the scale and look of the original house, repeat the pitch of the rooflines on the addition. Size and height of the new roofs may vary; but with similar slopes, harmony will reign.
- **Materials.** Matching new and old materials produces a unified look; but if your house is brick or some other kind of stone, this approach could be exorbitantly expensive. Fortunately, complementary or contrasting materials look good, too, provided the colors are in the same range and the trim matches. For example, using wood siding on the gable ends or dormers of a brick house could provide a design precedent for cladding the addition in wood siding.
- **Architectural Elements.** Another harmonizing strategy— match the scale and shape of existing windows and doors, and repeat design details such as shutters, side lites, and trim above windows and doors and at rooflines. Do you want extra-large windows in the addition? Match them to the smaller originals by trimming them the same way or installing grilles that echo the existing mullions. Other ways to link old and new structures—a breezeway that connects the two or a wide patio or pergola that pulls the two parts together.

ABOVE
Making a transition between kitchen and garden, this little addition offers a place to sit, arrange flowers, or deposit muddy boots.

OPPOSITE
If you frequently entertain large groups of friends and family, adding a dining room may be a good investment for you.

smart tip REALITY CHECK

Before you get carried away with ideas for more living space, remember that any changes you make will affect your existing house—how it looks and how it functions. For example:

■ Will the addition meet the needs of everyone in the household, including extended family and guests. Will it be accessible to those with special needs?

■ Will it meet future needs as well as present ones?

■ How will the addition affect traffic flow within the house, the amount of natural lighting received indoors, exterior views, and access to the outdoors?

■ With the addition in place, will you need to make changes to landscaping, walkways, or the driveway?

■ Will the addition increase demands on existing plumbing, electrical, heating, and ventilation services? Are all of these services adequate to handle it?

“ It took us 10 years...but it was worth

ADDITION RENOVATION
case study

AFTER

Doing most of the work themselves—and saving a lot of money in the process—Mark and Lucianna Samu revitalized the exterior of this Long Island, New York, carriage house, transforming it from dowdy to dandy with relatively minor alterations.

The house, built in 1880 to contain the horses and carriages for a large estate, was beginning to look a little shabby on the outside when the couple bought it, but for the first few years they gave most of their attention to the interiors, working on the outside a little at a time. "It took us 10 years to do the exterior," says Mark, "but it was worth the wait." Taken together, all of their improvements lifted the house out of its design doldrums and gave it crisp charm and architectural presence. They began the transformation by scraping years of cracking and peeling paint from the clapboards and giving them a fresh coat of white paint. Most of the windows were in place when the Samus bought the house. "They were adequate," says Mark. "We decided that replacing them would be too expensive, so we caulked and painted and generally spruced them up." They did, however remove some plain-Jane windows at one end of the house, replacing them with a lucky find of two 18-in.-wide French doors, which they installed as fixed glass. Working on the upgrade of an old house, Lucianna, a designer and space planner, found the vintage windows in a trash heap and brought them home. Then, to make two small upstairs spaces a little bigger and airier, they added two dormers,

BEFORE

one of which expands a bedroom; the other enlarges a landing at the top of the stairs. Although the gabled dormers measure only 12 square feet each, they improved living space inside and added great distinction to the exterior. The entrance came next. The existing one not only lacked distinction but had no overhang to protect friends and family from the elements. To remedy both problems, the Samus opened up the hipped-roof dormer above the front door with a large round-topped window and bumped the dormer out 2 feet so that it hangs over the front steps. The overhang, supported by four stately columns, gives the facade great distinction, extends a friendly welcome to visitors, and is large enough to create a little porch, which provides shelter for the front door. New steps heighten the impact of the updated entryway. The window in the large dormer is set back a couple of feet, allowing for a little balcony, which this busy couple rarely gets a chance to use. "We've sat on it maybe twice," says Mark, "but we do hang Christmas lights out there every year."

the wait. "

design workbook
NEW GABLE DORMERS ADD STYLE

curb appeal

The addition of new dormers, a balcony, and an imposing entry dresses up the tired facade of this hundred-year-old carriage house.

detailed dormers

To unify the front facade, all of the new dormers feature muntins and other period-style details, such as traditional trim. (See also top far left and left.)

elegant entry

Using some salvaged materials cut costs, allowing a splurge on a high-quality paneled door (far left), which suits the style of the building.

classy columns

Using cardboard cutouts, the owners played with the size and shape of the columns. "We'd walk away and look at them from all angles until they were just right."

66 Now there's a nice view when you get

AFTER

ADDITION RENOVATION
case study

BEFORE

O ne of the new gables that punctuates the roof of Mark and Lucianna Samu's Long Island carriage house (see the Case Study and Design Workbook on page 142–145) encloses a cozy window seat piled high with pillows. The gable is positioned at the top of the stairs, where it replaces a blank wall, and functions as a little landing. The gable window ushers some welcome daylight into the formerly dark space; and, says Samu, "Now there's a nice view when you get to the top of the stairs." But the landing is more than just a pretty place. A deep drawer under the window seat stores pillows, blankets, and other items too bulky to fit into the linen closet and a roomy cabinet tucked into the side wall also provides storage. As with any type of dormer, the pitch of the roof determined the amount of floor space inside with usable headroom. If the Samus had added a shed dormer to their home, they would have gained more floor space because the structure isn't limited by a double-pitched gable roof. It would have been easier to frame, too. But aesthetically, the gable style looks best with the architecture of the house, and so that was important to these homeowners.

In the end, the couple used the new interior space they gained creatively by building cabinetry into the knee walls (the space under the pitched roofline) and by creating the window seats that have deep storage drawers beneath them. Remember, the size, number, and location of the dormers have a major effect on the space they shelter.

If you are thinking about adding gable dormers to your home, consider multiples. Groups of two or more small dormers look better on the outside than one, and the more you deploy, the more usable space you'll get inside. Another thing to consider about adding dormers is that you will have to try to match the new siding and roofing material to that on the existing structure—unless you plan to re-side or repaint, and install a new roof over the entire house after the addition is complete. And the right trimwork is as important as the right siding. Good detailing at corners, roof edges, and windows counts, too. Not only will it affect the addition's appearance, but it is crucial to keeping water and weather outside. However, adding dormers, especially gabled ones, gives you the opportunity, as it did the Samus, to banish a monotonous flat roofline and create dynamic space inside your house with views from on high.

to the top ... "

design workbook
ADD ON AND BUMP OUT

great heights

A vaulted ceiling keeps this kitchen addition from looking boxy. Skylights and lots of windows keep it bright. (See also top left.)

exterior enhancement

A glass bump-out (top left) provides a sunny eating space and access to the yard. Its pitched roof gives interest to the addition's exterior appearance.

character building

Salvaged posts and beams and exposed rafters bring a sense of age and architectural character to the new interior space. (See also bottom left.)

coordinated effort

Antique cabinets (far left) blend beautifully with the vintage look of the room. They inspired the design of the new cabinetry on the opposite side of the center island (left).

6

exterior makeovers

PAINT   ARCHITECTURAL DETAILS
SIDING   ROOFING   LANDSCAPING   CASE STUDIES:
INTERVIEWS AND DESIGN WORKBOOKS

Do the words "curb appeal" conjure up images of hasty upgrades and feverish real-estate transactions? If so, it's no wonder—sprucing up a house to attract potential buyers is, in fact, one reason to undertake an exterior remodel. But another, perhaps more important, reason is to please yourself and enhance your enjoyment of your home, outside as well as inside. Your interior living spaces may look great, but if your heart sinks every time you pull into the driveway and look up, it's time to make some changes. Don't worry, exterior improvements don't have to be expensive or complicated; you can do some of them yourself in a weekend. Simple changes can make a big difference. For instance, cleaning up the front yard, cutting back ungainly, overgrown shrubs, and planting a bunch of perky annuals are quick fixes with big impact.

This house, once old and shabby, now makes a good impression. All it took was a coat of crisp white paint.

Adding trim to featureless windows and doors can also create new architectural appeal in a hurry, and painting that trim rather than investing in an entire paint job may be enough for a fresh new look.

How do you know you need an upgrade? The same way you know when it's time for a facelift. You can usually tell by looking. If you're unsure, your friends, with any encouragement at all, will tell you. Ask them. You can also ask a real estate broker, even if you're not interested in selling at this time. Roger Hillstrom, a sales agent for Frank Lumia Real Estate Plus in Delhi, New York, says it's quite acceptable to approach a real-estate professional and say, "I'm not ready to sell right now but if I were, how would you assess the outside of my house? Does it need improvement? What would you suggest?" If an agent expects to get a listing in the future he or she will be honest and forthright with suggestions, says Hillstrom.

To do your own appraisal, walk around your house, looking it over with a critical eye. You might take a camera with you, snapping pictures of areas that look problematic. First, check the overall appearance. How does it stand up to the houses up and down the street? Be ruthless. Pretend you are a potential buyer and make notes of the things that would turn you off—shabby siding, missing roof shingles, peeling paint, unruly shrubbery, and the like. Has your house been done up in outdated paint colors? Does it present a hodgepodge of warring architectural styles? Have certain key architectural elements worn out or been removed? You may discover that one or more of these conditions exist, but don't worry—all of them are fixable. Find inspiration for your exterior improvements in the projects that follow.

paint

Unless you do it yourself, a paint job will set you back several thousand dollars at least, more if your house is very large or has lots of windows, doors, porches, and detailing. But you'll get a big bang for those bucks—applying paint color is the quickest and simplest way to change the look of your house, giving it new flair; highlighting its architectural details; making it look bigger, smaller, taller, or wider; blending it into its surroundings; or making it stand out. Even a minor upgrade, such as painting just the millwork around windows and doors, will have a major uplifting effect. Unless you want to paint frequently, avoid trendy colors that are "in" at the moment. They'll be "out" soon, and your house will look dated. Or if you must use a trendy color, restrict it to the trim

ABOVE
Let the paint color you choose express your personal tastes and enhance the character of your house. Bright blue enlivens this Victorian farmhouse, and white makes its intricate trim pop.

OPPOSITE
Deep red, reminiscent of barns all over America, looks great on any traditionally styled frame house. Here, curlicue architectural detailing on the front gable adds a bit of whimsy.

ABOVE
Soft, neutral beige is just right for this modest cottage. A brick path and an exuberant garden add texture and color.

OPPOSITE
Pale apple-green paint, white gingerbread trim, and a picket fence make this rambling Victorian look its best.

so that it's easy to redo in a couple of years when those "hot" house colors grow cold.

But does it really need a paint job? Maybe your house just needs a good bath. Before you hire a painter, wipe down a section of the siding with a soapy sponge. This little test may reveal that an accumulation of dirt and dust is the problem. If so, refresh wood siding by washing it with a mixture of one cup of strong detergent and one quart of bleach in three gallons of water. The bleach will help remove mold; an alternative is a mildewcide, available from your local paint dealer. Wear gloves; scrub from the top down with a long-handled, soft-bristled brush; rinse thoroughly with the garden hose before the cleaning solution dries; and change the wash mixture frequently. Power-washing, which you can do yourself or hire out to a professional, is another option, but be careful—too much pressure can damage the wood and even remove paint.

A good washing may be what's needed to give vinyl or aluminum siding a bright new look, too. In fact, experts advise that a spray-wash with your garden hose once a year will keep these materials looking their best for a long time. If you wait longer than a year, you will probably need to do some scrubbing with a cleaning solution. If that doesn't do the trick, both vinyl and aluminum can also be painted. But check with the manufacturer of your siding before you proceed; some will void their warranties if their product is painted.

Paints that adhere successfully to vinyl are relatively new, and experts recommend using a color that is no darker than the current shade. If you're tired of the beige vinyl siding you have now, you can choose a pale sage green or white or light blue, but darker colors will absorb the heat of the sun, causing the siding to warp and interfering with the paint's ability to adhere. Before you paint either vinyl or aluminum yourself, get good advice from your paint dealer—success depends on carefully preparing the surface and using the right paint and primer.

Choosing Color

If you decide to paint, you're in for a treat. Nothing has a greater design impact than color on the exterior of your house. And because the colors you choose should express your taste and personality, you'll have fun shopping for house paint. But before you go with purple because it's your favorite hue, think about some other things, too. There are no "rules" for exterior paint

make a perfect match

Some homeowners prefer an exterior color scheme that coordinates with the palette they've chosen for the interior spaces of their home. However, the best way to determine how your house colors will come together in one perfect palette for all of the exterior elements—the siding, trim, door, shutters, and even the roofing material—is to see them in front of you. If you want to be very high-tech, there are computer programs available that will put all of the colors together for you. But simpler methods are just as effective and a lot more personally satisfying. Draw a sketch of your house, and make several photocopies. Then use colored pencils to add in the details. Later, you can get paint chips of all the colors and look at them together, but for an initial overall picture, informal colored sketches work fine.

Most houses will have some fixed features that can help determine the color direction you should take. Look at the roof, for example. Whether it is covered in slate, asphalt shingles, terra-cotta tile, metal, or something else, the roof is a large visible surface, and its color should coordinate with the color of the facade. Unless you plan to paint over brickwork or natural siding, add its color (or a close representation) to your palette. Additional masonry features, such as front stairs, walls, walkways, and driveways, should be accounted for on your sketch, too. And don't overlook the foundation or the foliage. Finally, just as a guideline, put a representative sampling of your neighbors' house colors in the margins of your sketch.

ABOVE
If a whole-house paint job isn't in your budget, just slap a warm color—like this bright yellow—on the front door.

OPPOSITE
Repeating the strong architectural symmetry of the house, this colonnaded entry porch reaches out to welcome visitors.

color, but the hues you choose will look best if they complement the architectural style of your house. Is it a Victorian, a bungalow, or a funky contemporary? If so, you can get away with a vibrant scheme that might include purple in small doses. But a vivid color palette applied to an orderly style such as Greek Revival or Federal could compromise the beauty and form of the architecture. Consider neutral or subdued colors instead.

Whether to paint or stain wood siding is an aesthetic choice. Today's latex paints and stains offer the same degree of protection for siding as alkyd-based coatings and will hold up for a number of years. If your house has natural-wood siding that you want to show off, you have a few staining options. You could use a clear sealant, which has no pigment. Otherwise, to retain the appearance of the wood grain but alter the color, you could try a semitransparent stain. This product is color-tinted, but just enough so that the grain of the wood is still apparent.

Another tip from the experts—avoid a scheme that clashes with the neighbors. If your house stands out like a sore thumb, it will not harmonize with its surroundings, and, say real estate experts, it may even prove difficult to sell. You don't have to slavishly copy nearby houses, but use restraint in your efforts to make your own home look distinctive.

To choose a color, leaf through magazines and design books and go for a drive, looking at houses you like. When you've come up with a candidate or two, walk around your house, visualizing how it will look done up in that color. Will it blend nicely with the roof, the foundation and other stonework, the porch, paths and walkways, flowers and shrubs, and nearby

houses? If you have a couple of favorite hues, go through this process with all of them.

But don't stop there. See how your chosen colors look on the house. Color chips won't be much help. Instead, buy the smallest possible container of your color candidates (some paint dealers will sell you a pint), and splash each shade on the house, front, sides, and back, in the sun and in the shade. If you've selected trim and accent colors, add those, too, so you can see what they all look like together. Many paint dealers offer color cards that suggest complementary combinations. Look at these colors for a few days many times a day to be sure you like them as the light changes from morning to noon to dusk.

OPPOSITE

A round window smartens up this gable end, acting as a focal point for the facade of the little house. Columns supporting the roof of a tiny porch also add interest.

ABOVE

Architectural trim is readily available at home centers for reasonable prices. Adding period details, as the owners of this house did, can make a huge improvement in the look of the exterior.

architectural details

The addition of architectural millwork can transform a drab house to a dazzling one in a hurry. You may live in an older house that's missing some of its original trim—and its charm—because previous owners removed it or time and weather destroyed it. Or perhaps your house is new but essentially featureless. In either case, embellishment can make a big difference. Top the windows with decorative arches; enliven a front porch with decorative railings and balusters; add brackets under the eaves. Thanks to the variety and accessibility of stock millwork, you can achieve handsome results easily and economically.

smart tip

COLOR EXPERTISE

If you can't decide on a color scheme for the exterior of your house or if you're unsure of the colors you've chosen, consult a color specialist. It may cost a few hundred dollars, but this investment can save you thousands if you have to repaint because you've made a hideous mistake. Ask your paint contractor to recommend someone, or consult an in-store expert.

Architectural trim is available in factory-made pieces that replicate eighteenth- and nineteenth-century designs; you can buy it in wood or in synthetic materials that stand up better than wood to wear and tear and rarely need maintenance. For purists, the original wood pieces themselves can be found at architectural salvage yards. To study the possibilities, get brochures and millwork catalogs through the mail, on the Internet, or from a home center.

Trim pieces vary from simple window and door moldings and shutters to roof brackets, pilasters, and columns—to elaborate embellishments such as gable dormers and cupolas.

Sprucing Up an Entry

Architectural trimwork can add character to your home, but the best and possibly the easiest place to start adding design interest is at the front door. Besides upgrading the appearance of your house, a new front door can help reinforce its architectural style. And it doesn't have to cost a lot. A door with leaded-glass panels will be expensive, yes, but embellishing the architecture around a plain door with handsome molding or other ornamentation will add character more economically. Even just painting the door a bold hue that coordinates with the rest of your scheme can add plenty of pizzazz.

ABOVE
The owners of this Victorian cottage were thrilled to find a vintage door and antique hardware at a salvage yard.

OPPOSITE
A clean-lined door with outstanding trim—a built-up crosshead and fluted pilasters—adds character to this home's simple facade.

dressing up a front door

Does your old front door need TLC? That means a new paint job for starters. If the door has been painted many times, take it off its hinges and strip it before adding more layers of paint. You will have to strip it if you intend to display the original wood. If you can get away with just painting the door, sand it down first and use an exterior latex paint or a stain. Once you've got the door itself spruced up, you can fit it with new hardware, a knocker, or even new glass. Another way to restore a door is to replace the casing—the trim that conceals the gap between the doorjambs and the walls. You can opt for a built-up crosshead—a heavier, detailed horizontal molding that goes over the door and pilasters (right)—and simulated pillars that run along the sides of the door. Some molding manufacturers offer pieces that eliminate the need for any difficult miter cuts.

It's best to choose a door that is consistent with the over-all design of your home. Wood doors are readily available, as are energy-efficient steel and fiberglass models that do not rot, warp, or buckle as wood does. And because these newer materials can be stained or painted, they can replicate the look of wood.

The consistency rule applies to all the other trim you may choose, as do the principles of harmony, proportion, and scale. Honor the essential character of your house, and avoid mixing distinct styles from different periods. Elaborate millwork will be all wrong on a 1950s ranch house, and a Victorian with no detail-ing at all will fade into architectural obscurity.

Study pictures of houses like yours in books and maga-zines, particularly ones that are chock full of images of architec-tural styles from Colonial times to the present. As you peruse them, you will find a house that is similar to yours, complete with the appropriate architectural detailing. Books are also helpful guides to restoring millwork missing from an older house. Check local historical records in the local library, too—you may turn up pictures of your own house in all of its original glory.

smart tip
HOUSE NUMBERS
Look online or in specialty shops for nifty house numbers, which come in many finishes and styles to match your home's architectural style. Remember that a sharp con-trast—dark numbers against a light surface or vice-versa—is best.

siding

Paint or power-cleaning may be enough to bring shabby or neglected siding up to speed, but serious damage calls for more stringent measures. In a nutshell—when siding is no longer protecting and weatherproofing the building and adding stability to the frame, it's time to do major repair work or choose a replacement material. This will be a costly project, but it can completely rejuvenate your home's exterior look.

OPPOSITE FAR LEFT
Replace damaged millwork, but match the architecture. Today, reproductions of vintage styles are easy to find.

OPPOSITE TOP
A front porch update will expand usable living space, improve the look of your home's exterior, and upgrade its resale value.

ABOVE
If fresh paint or power washing aren't enough to significantly improve the look of your siding, it's time to replace it.

To evaluate the condition of wood siding, look for cracked or rotting boards. Deteriorated areas allow moisture to penetrate to the framing, which in time will produce rot. In masonry or stucco, cracks are the culprits. You can probably fix a couple of bad spots yourself—repairs or patches to wood or masonry can be blended smoothly into the existing siding, and wood shingles and shakes can be easily replaced. Damage to aluminum or vinyl siding, however, which usually appears in the form of dents or actual breaks, presents some challenges and is best handled by a professional. If the problem spots in any kind of siding are extensive, you may need to consider re-siding the house. If it's time to replace your siding, you've got many materials from which to choose.

■ **Wood.** Favored by many people for its natural beauty and traditional appearance, wood has some drawbacks. It requires periodic maintenance, must be repainted every five to ten years, and is susceptible to damage from moisture, termites, and fire. And with lumber prices climbing higher and higher, re-siding with wood has become an expensive proposition.

■ **Vinyl.** Many people, tired of the frequent maintenance that wood siding requires, choose vinyl instead. Popular for its insulating and waterproofing qualities, vinyl is a low-maintenance material and resistant to rust. Vinyl siding has come a long way aesthetically in recent years: more colors and architectural trim pieces are available, and in some brands, the color goes all the way through the material for a more realistic look. And vinyl siding is no longer limited to clapboard look-alikes; there are also vinyl shingles, shakes, and logs that mimic the look of natural wood.

■ **Engineered Wood.** Also known as composite wood, this type of siding is made up of wood particles bound together by resins. Available in the form of clapboards and shingles with a wood-grain finish, it comes already primed, can be painted and costs less than natural wood.

■ **Fiber Cement.** A relatively new siding material, fiber cement also mimics the look of wood clapboards and is less costly. Composed of cement, sand, and cellulose fiber, it is durable, non-combustible, and requires little maintenance.

■ **Manufactured Stone.** Also called cast stone, this type of siding is showing up more and more often on new houses and

LEFT
Many older houses are distinguished by walls of rich-looking natural stone. Manufactured stone, an economical alternative, is widely available for new house construction and can also be used to repair older stone houses.

roofing

as a replacement siding material for older houses. Made of cement, stone aggregates, and iron oxide pigments, it is poured into molds that replicate stucco and many types of stone, can be installed over wood, concrete, or masonry block, and is priced competitively with hard-coat stucco.

You may need an expert opinion on whether to repair or re-side your house. If so, choose a professional carefully, opting for a local reputable firm that has done satisfactory work for people you know.

And if re-siding is in your immediate future, be sure you get complete information from your contractor about all of the materials that are available and which ones will stand up best to the climate in your area. Some materials do particularly well in hot, dry climates; some are engineered to withstand snow, rain, and humidity. Also check local codes for any restrictions.

Inspect your roof in the early spring right after snow and ice have melted and winter damage is easy to spot. If your inspection reveals serious problems, contact roofing contractors in the spring, too, giving them time to submit bids, and giving yourself time to check references and talk to previous customers. Another reason to get right on it—roofing costs may increase substantially if you wait until late spring or early summer.

As you conduct your inspection, keep an eagle eye out for sags in the roof; missing, damaged, or worn shingles or tiles; hard or brittle shingles; and bald spots. Other potential problems—loose or popped nails, loose or missing flashing, and algae growth. Test for rot by poking at the eave shingles with the tip of a screwdriver: if you can push it in more than a half-inch water has probably penetrated into the framing and is threatening the integrity of the structure. On metal roofs, rust is a red

flag. Roof damage is not always obvious from the outside. Take a trip to the attic or crawl space, too, looking for water stains in rafters, insulation, and sheathing.

If the problems you spot are not extensive—and your roof is less than 10 or 15 years old—simple repairs are probably adequate, and you may be able to do these yourself. But if you notice damage to most of the shingles or a noticeable sag in the roof profile, you'll need extensive repairs or possibly a new roof, best installed by a pro. Hiring a roofing contractor could add as much as 50 percent to the job, but it may beat doing it yourself. Roofing is tiring, time-consuming, and potentially dangerous; and it requires a certain amount of skill. If you don't do it right, you'll pay for it. It might be worth paying a professional.

If you must replace your roof, choose the new material carefully, making sure that it blends with the color and architecture of your house and is suitable for your climate. There are a number of choices for your consideration.

■ **Asphalt, or Composition Roofing.** The most common and least expensive roofing material, asphalt also offers the most variety in color and texture and offers a 15- to 30-year lifespan. Asphalt shingles show their age when the protective granule coating begins to wear off, revealing the black asphalt underneath. Curling and cracking on the corners of shingles indicate that the roof has begun to wear out and lose its weatherproof seal. Architectural shingles, which are slightly more expensive, have a more substantial look and in certain colors resemble shakes or even slate.

■ **Wood Shingles and Shakes.** Considered the roofing of choice for Cape Cod, Shingle-style, bungalow, and other traditional architectural styles, wood shingles and shakes are more expensive than asphalt, more time-consuming to install, and more maintenance intensive. Because they are combustible, they are not a good choice for areas prone to fires, such as Southern California, Texas, or Oklahoma.

■ Metal Roofing. Once used predominantly on utility or commercial buildings, metal roofing is showing up more and more in residential neighborhoods. It's long lasting and available in a variety of baked-on-enamel colors. Beware of galvanized-metal sheets, which do not stand up as well as other metals, however. Metal roofing with the look of clay tile and wood shakes is also available.

■ Clay and Concrete Tiles. Tiles give Mediterranean-style houses their distinctive look. They're long-lasting but heavy, and require an underpinning that can handle a heavy load.

OPPOSITE
Tile roofs are most often used on Mediterranean- and Spanish-style houses. These tiles, like many other natural roofing materials, are available today in realistic-looking man-made versions.

ABOVE
A simple garden bordered by a low picket fence is an apt accompaniment to this Shingle-style house. A more formal garden would have compromised the casual cottage look of the house.

■ **Slate.** A slate roof can last for generations; it sheds ice and snow beautifully and offers a rich traditional look. On the downside—slate is costly and heavy, and it requires an extra-strong roof structure.

■ **Alternative Materials.** A sand-cement mixture, fiber-reinforced cement, acrylic resins bonded to metal, rubber, and other recycled materials are now readily available in forms that mimic the look of conventional roofs. Ask your lumberyard or roofing contractor about them.

landscaping

If you're an enthusiastic and talented gardener you can probably spruce up your property with new trees, shrubs, and flowers—and have a lot of fun doing it. Not particularly gifted? Short on time? Call for help. Landscape or garden designers, who are often employed by large nurseries, can help you select and install plants that are appropriate to your area. For a major project, however, such as establishing an extensive new garden, putting in a pool, or correcting the contours of your site, a landscape architect is the person to call. These professionals are also helpful if you're clueless about what kind of improvements need to be made in the first place.

"Landscape architects are trained to do many things, from creating gardens to solving drainage problems to installing outdoor living areas," says Jeffrey N. Hartt, an Albany, New York, landscape architect. "All of those projects," she adds, "increase

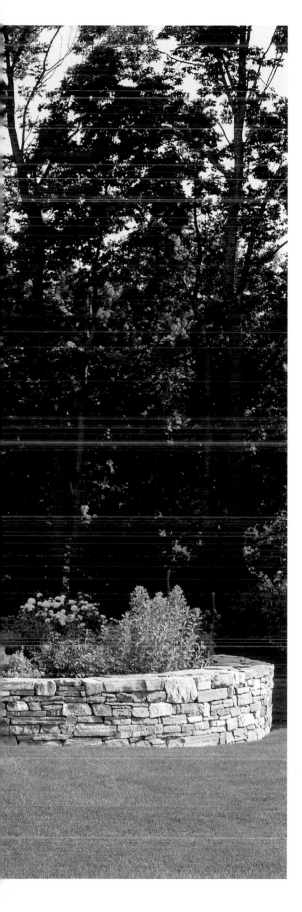

the value of a home as well as harmonizing it with its site and enhancing the indoor space with views of the landscape.

"Our worlds are enriched and our perspectives broadened," says Hartt, "by the world outside our windows—a flower garden, birds darting in a woodland border, and glimpses of a distant field in the sunlight."

Hartt advises homeowners to approach a landscaping project systematically by creating a wish list, then hiring the landscape architect to conduct a site analysis, develop a site plan, and provide a cost estimate. Once you and the landscape architect agree on the scope and details of the project, he or she will oversee installation by a qualified landscape contractor. If you're willing to do the digging and planting yourself, you'll cut costs considerably.

The cost of a landscaping project is difficult to estimate without an on-site analysis by a professional, but one rule of thumb (which may vary greatly from one area of the country to another) suggests that the fee for a created landscape amounts to about ten percent of the worth of the property but adds 15 percent to its resale value.

If a landscaping project is not in your budget, you can still make a positive impact on your property by planting some shrubs or trees at the front; enhancing your entry with a walkway and a decorative urn full of flowers; hanging flower boxes from your windows or porch railings. For ideas, visit your local nurseries and study gardening books and magazines.

Lighting the Landscape

You've brought your house out of the design doldrums, and it looks great. To prevent it from fading back into the shadows once the sun sets, consider the benefits of outdoor lighting.

Architectural, or accent, lighting creates outdoor interest and drama by highlighting the design of your house or the landscaping around it, or both. It may accentuate the overall architecture or focus on a particularly handsome feature such as a colonnaded entry or a textured wall. Properly positioned lighting can also draw attention to a graceful tree or a lush bed of shrubbery, or even direct a wash of light toward a stone wall or fence.

Of course, for safety and security purposes you'll want to be sure that all walkways, stairs, porches, and entry doors are properly lit. And to beef up security you may want to consider combining your outdoor lighting with devices that sense motion

TOP LEFT
Classical columns, a paneled wood door, and a period pendant-syle light fixture all contribute to the glamour of this stately entry.

LEFT
Recessed fixtures installed in the soffits illuminate the exterior, and cast dramatic pools of light downward.

OPPOSITE
After the sun sets, indoor and outdoor lighting work together to highlight and dramatize the architecture of this house.

how to use outdoor lighting effectively

Vary lighting effects for maximum impact. *Uplighting* casts a pool of light upward. *Downlighting* does the opposite. Use them alone or together for contrast against a surface. Uplighting alone can provide fairly wide coverage of shrubbery in a border or against the foundation. Installed at the bottom of a tree, it can illuminate the upper branches. Downlighting alone is excellent for safety, and it's often used to brighten an entry and along paths and stairways. *Spotlighting* is more specific, casting a narrow beam of light on an object. Spotlighting is always done from a distance. To highlight something and eliminate shadows, you will have to

light it from several directions. But if you choose to make use of the shadows and patterns created by light, try *backlighting,* which will project interesting silhouettes onto a surface.

To emphasize texture, such as that of a stone wall, a fence, grillwork, or foliage, lighting professionals use a technique called *grazing*. The fixture is placed close to the surface and aimed at a 45-degree angle. For an even wash of light, fixtures can be installed further away from the surface. This is referred to as *wall washing*.

Another technique, *moonlighting,* casts light down from several points in a tree.

If you don't need the formal training and expertise of a landscape architect—or can't afford one—a landscape designer or garden designer may be the ticket. Although not regulated or accredited, garden designers are generally conversant with the plants that grow well in your area and can work with you to draw up a garden plan or create a working drawing for a landscape contractor to follow. Any of these professionals know how trees, shrubs, and plants will look year-round and how they will harmonize with your existing garden. Large nurseries often employ landscape designers, garden designers, and even horticulturists.

Landscape contractors install gardens and garden features such as fences, walls, or water features that a homeowner, landscape architect, or landscape designer has designed. They also build or oversee the building of outdoor living areas, swimming pools, and tennis courts. Many landscape contractors also handle maintenance jobs such as weeding, pest control, mulching, mowing, watering, and fertilizing.

Step 3 SELECT A SPECIALIST

Although you will save money by hiring your brother-in-law to paint your house or put on a roof, you may not be happy with the results over time. Wherever you live, there are bound to be many home-improvement specialists who have years of experience and, equally important, know what sort of paint and siding and roofing materials will perform best in your part of the country.

Check out these people as carefully as you would any other home-improvement professional—interview several candidates, asking for references and insurance information, and be sure to get a contract that spells out dates, details, and a payment schedule. See Chapter 1 for more details on this process.

ABOVE AND OPPOSITE
Before remodeling, this dormer was punctuated with one tiny window, giving a top-heavy feel to the exterior and limiting the amount of light that entered. To solve both problems, the owners carved out space in the dormer for a large window. (See Chapter 5, pages 142–145, for more information about this project.)

why use a landscape architect?

Here is what an landscape architect can do for your home:

- Enhance the welcoming quality of your home's front elevation and entry
- Establish perennial, woodland, vegetable, and other types of gardens
- Provide areas for outdoor recreation—pools, tennis courts, children's playgrounds

- Create outdoor living, cooking, and dining spaces
- Reinforce pleasant views and screen unsightly views
- Create outdoor privacy
- Improve outdoor circulation patterns—walkways, steps and landings, parking
- Solve drainage problems
- Change the contours of the landscape
- Increase the resale value of your house
- Develop an outdoor lighting plan

design workbook
DRAMATIC TRANSFORMATION

enhanced facade

A dynamic new look for the exterior of a bland old ranch house derives from the new built-out entry, a new roof, columns, and a rock wall.

unifiying elements

To unite old and new sections of the house, the architect repeated the columns that frame the entry and specified pop-in muntins for the windows.

added detail

A gray-stone wall and border, top left, extends across most of the home's front elevation and adds much-needed interest to the facade.

architectural accent

Panes of glass in the new paneled oak door, left, echo the grid pattern on the entry gable and windows. Its Arts and Crafts styling makes an architectural statement.

" We loved the house, the long deep

EXTERIOR RENOVATION
case study

BEFORE

AFTER

Amy and John Donnelly say that their 1913 Sears Arts & Crafts kit house looked a "little funky" when they first saw it, but they could see the charm underneath. In an extensive remodel that took several years to complete, they updated parts of the house themselves. Then three children later, they finished the job with the help of an architect and a remodeling contractor, doubling the square footage of the house to make room for their growing family.

Their first step was to find an architect who specialized in Arts & Crafts-style houses. "We did all the right things—got referrals, interviewed several people, checked references, looked at completed work," says Amy. "Some friends gave us the name of Xiomara Paredes, and coincidentally, she was at the same time recommended by an expensive architect in town who thought our job was too small for him. As it turned out, her portfolio was full of Arts & Crafts houses."

Lots of architects looked at the project, but Amy and Paredes, whose architectural practice is in Glen Rock, New Jersey, really clicked. "She listened to us," recalls Amy. "On her first visit, she went through the house and gave me ideas. The other architects didn't do that—one refused to share his ideas until I'd paid him. Her enthusiasm for our house and what we wanted to do was a key selling point. We weren't looking for someone who just wanted a job." The Donnellys had a positive experience with their contractor, too.

They interviewed a number of people and then chose Tony Visaggio of Antique Creations Inc. in Park Ridge, New Jersey, who had done an addition for their neighbors. "We were impressed with his work and with the personal guarantee he gives to every project," says John. "For example, he returned four years later to fix—at his own expense—a path at our neighbors' house that had settled 'funny.' " Another plus—he and the architect worked well together, solving problems as they came up.

The Donnellys focused on the outside of the original house first, replacing Arts & Crafts details that had been removed, such as a window in a dormer above the front door. They updated the inside, too, doing most of the work themselves. When their third child was born they considered moving. "But we loved the house, the long deep yard, the town, our neighbors—so we decided to stay put and add on," they say. The original two-bedroom 1,800-square-foot house now has five bedrooms and 3,600 sq. ft. As the addition unfolded, the couple paid great attention to architectural details outside as well as in—all the doors, windows, moldings, even the porch lights and the front-door handle and lockset are faithful period reproductions.

Through their research they also discovered a two-tone color scheme that is appropriate to the period. Today the house looks fresh and bright but still retains the charm of the 1913 original. Although their remodeling experience was essentially positive, the Donnellys do have a few regrets. The late delivery of custom windows and doors increased the stress because it meant that parts of the house were exposed to cold winter air. During a major remodeling, they both agree, "it's better to spend the extra money to live elsewhere." But they also advise that it's important to be involved in the project and be at the job site often.

yard, the town, our neighbors..."

design workbook
RESPECT FOR THE PAST

the right stuff

Arts and Crafts-style windows are reproductions, but the grilles have the right period look, as do the paint colors that uplift this 1913 beauty.

details, details

Sconces, top far left, flanking the side door—now the main entry—have unevenly tinted glass. A verdigris finish graces them with a patina of age.

and more details

The owners searched a long time for the right handle and lockset, top left. It's a faithful reproduction of an Arts and Crafts model.

true to character

Another authentic reproduction, the oak door and its features—the color of the stain, the grille, sidelites, and transom—is faithful to the home's original architecture.

outdoor living

Now that you have updated both the interior and exterior of your house, why not look at your outdoor-living possibilities? Most of the projects involved are relatively inexpensive.

What is best for you? Perhaps a front porch where you can relax, read, sip a frosty glass of iced tea, and watch the world go by—even if it's raining? Maybe a backyard space would suit you best. Patios, placed near the house or set into a favorite spot in the garden, have a slightly formal charm. Decks, eminently economical to build, can be simple or elaborate; sunny, shady, or a little bit of both; small; or sprawling with several levels. And if your budget allows, you can install a complete outdoor kitchen where you can cook, serve, and clean up a gourmet meal without ever having to go into the house.

Relatively small changes to a patio, porch, or deck can extend your home's living space to the outdoors.

Your budget and the property on which your house sits will be important factors in determining the kind of outdoor living space you will build. But also take into account the existing landscaping, the architectural style of your home; the prevailing winds, sun, and shade; and the kinds of activities your outdoor oasis will accommodate. Look around your neighborhood for ideas; take snapshots of designs you particularly like; develop a portfolio of your notations, photos or drawings from magazines, and any advice you receive. This chapter will further clarify your needs and ideas and transform them into reality.

decks, patios, and porches

F ew outdoor-oasis projects are as appealing as decks. They offer an economical way to extend living space, even with today's skyrocketing lumber costs. They also promise almost instant gratification—simple ones can take as little as a day or two to complete; even some complex ones can be built in a week. For homeowners with carpentry skills and a little free time, a deck is a satisfying do-it-yourself project. And it will increase your home's resale value for a tiny fraction of what it would cost to add a front porch or put up an addition.

Ground-level decks, suitable for flat locations, resemble low platforms; they may extend living space by adjoining a house or sit freestanding wherever you want to put them. Because ground-level decks don't require railings (although you can certainly add them for visual interest or safety) or stairs, they are especially economical to build.

Sometimes the slope of a yard or the design of a house makes anything but a *raised deck* impractical. If your house has a walkout basement, a raised deck easily extends space from a living area, great room, or kitchen. And one flight up, a raised deck enhances the livability of a second-story bedroom. *Multilevel decks,* connected by steps or ramps, can follow the contours of a sloped lot. Sets of steps that connect one level to another provide a division between lounging, cooking, and eating areas. Multilevel decks also often devote one level to a hot tub or spa.

RIGHT
To make alfresco dining easy, build an outdoor kitchen on a patio or deck. Add a roof to guarantee all-weather enjoyment.

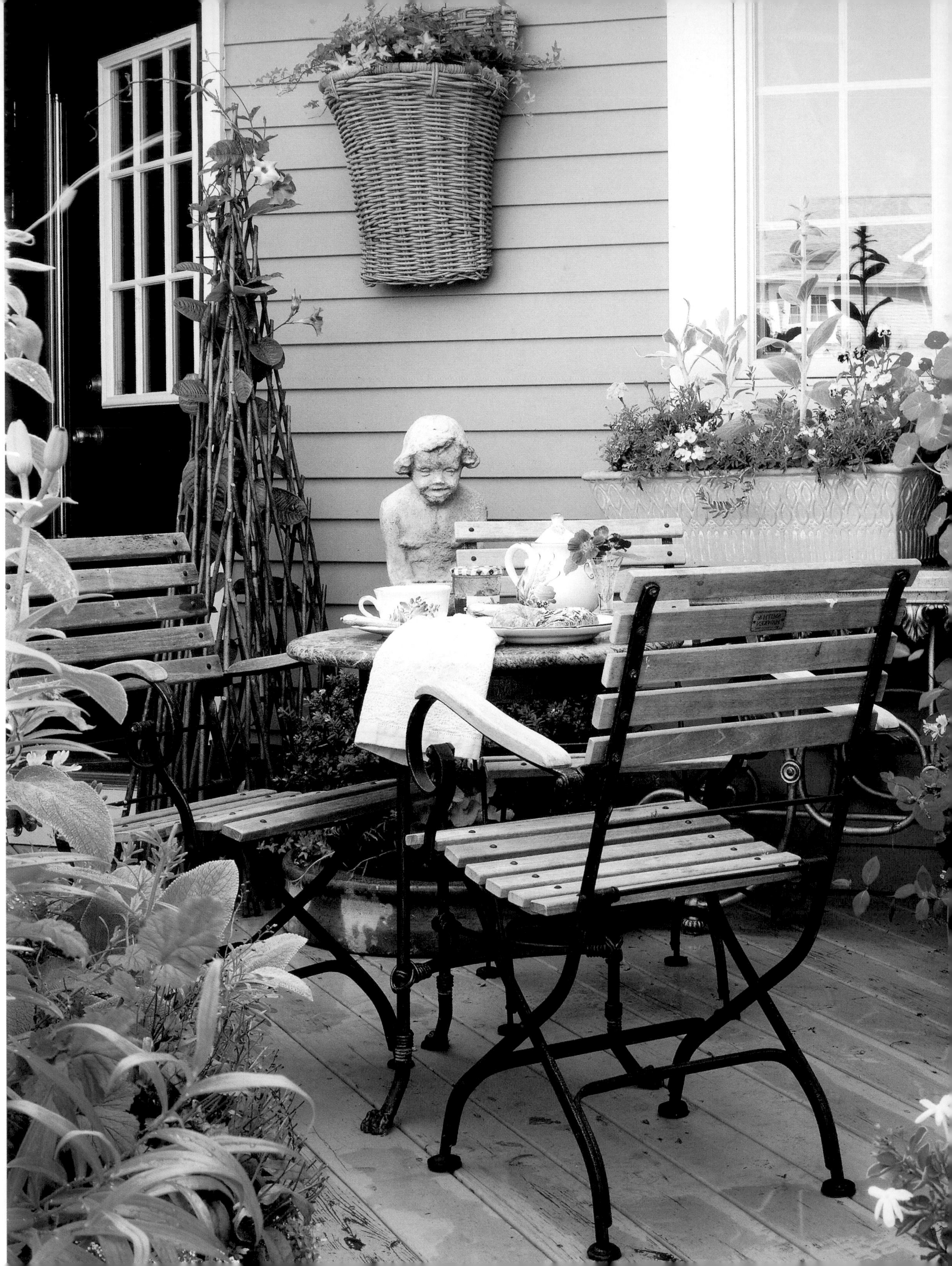

smart tip

DECK DESIGN SOFTWARE

Programs you can run on your home computer can help you organize your design ideas. Produced by a number of companies, the software makes simple work of drawing decks, railings, planters, and other deck amenities. Some versions show your work in three-dimensional rotating images that allow you to take a virtual tour of the deck and the surrounding area. The programs can also provide materials lists and building instructions.

Traditionally, decks have been built from wood—redwood, cedar, pressure-treated pine, or tropical hardwoods. Thanks to some recent technological developments, there are two new categories of decking—extruded vinyl and composite, which is made of natural fiber and recycled plastic. These engineered products are more expensive than wood initially and may require special installation techniques, but they offer significant savings over time because they require almost no maintenance.

Wood decks look best and last longer if they receive some protection from the elements. A water-repellent finish keeps the wood from shrinking or splintering, and a wood preservative slows down decay. Many people also apply paint or stain to a deck. Semitransparent stains let the wood grain show through; opaque stains and paint conceal the grain of the wood as well as its flaws.

Plan the size of your deck to accommodate the activities you envision taking place there. Is it just for sitting? It'll need space for only a few chairs and maybe a little table. But if you're going to cook, eat, and entertain, you'll need to build bigger. Think ahead so that the deck you end up with is roomy enough to fit the largest number of people you anticipate for an outdoor party—and strong enough to support them all. And factor in the weight should you want to outfit it with a hot tub or cooking and cooling appliances. To maximize space, consider building in cabinets and countertops, benches, tables, and planters.

LEFT

Eating open-air meals on a deck is one of the joys of summer. And decks are fun to decorate, too. Stained the same color as the house, this deck boasts stylish furniture and containers overflowing with plants, while a stone garden cherub looks on.

If you decide to take the do-it-your-self road, you'll find easy-to-follow plans on the Internet, in plans books or magazines, or at a local home center. If you'd rather turn the project over to a professional, chose someone who can provide design ideas as well as installation—an architect, house designer, or landscape architect; some landscaping contractors also design and install decks. Another approach is to hire a local carpenter to build from plans you have selected.

Patios

Unlike decks, most of which are attached to houses, patios can go anywhere in your backyard—directly adjoining a living room or first-floor master suite, just outside the kitchen, surrounding a pool, or sequestered in a shady, scenic part of the garden. A thoughtfully designed patio, no matter how small, makes a great escape in pleasant weather.

If you think of patios as boring hunks of concrete, think again. Paving has come a long way in recent years, and there are many materials from which to choose. Any of these materials—or a creative mix of them—can produce a great-looking outdoor oasis. And you don't need to stop at one; a couple of patios lushly landscaped, each oriented to a dif-

RIGHT
A table and chairs make this poolside patio a peaceful place for lunch. Umbrellas scattered around the area provide cool shade when the temperature rises.

OPPOSITE
Instead of putting down your patio right next to your house, take some time to walk around your property in search of the best location or great views.

ferent view, and connected by stone paths can make especially delightful outdoor living spaces.

Brick is an elegant traditional choice, but stone patio pavers are equally attractive. Generally more durable than brick, stone pavers include granite, sandstone, slate, quartzite, marble, and limestone. An economical alternative to natural stone, concrete pavers are available in a variety of sizes, and new methods of stamping poured concrete create patterns and textures that closely resemble real stone. Composite stone-look materials are also available; ask your local retailer or home center about them. Most of these materials are available in a range of earthy colors—grays, beiges, and rusts—and some even incorporate green and blue tones. Before you select a material, try to get a look at a hunk of the actual material; better yet, ask to see it used in a finished patio. Catalog or magazine photos don't always present an accurate picture. Also, ask your landscape designer, retailer, or home center what materials stand up best to the vagaries of the weather in your area.

Take time selecting a site for your patio. Notice where the sun rises and sets and estimate how much natural shade will be available at the times you're most likely to use it. Afraid it will be too sunny? Reposition the patio to take advantage of the shade from existing trees or a wall of your house—or plant some trees or large shrubs to create the shade you want.

Think also about the way you will use the patio and allow enough room for different types of seating (reclining and upright chairs) and tables (dining and occasional) you will need; if you will be cooking there, factor in the size of either a portable grill or built-in appliances. A fireplace is a smart amenity for the evening, and a water feature makes a nice addition; if you live in an urban area or on a busy suburban street, the sound of moving water can camouflage ambient noise.

select a site

Before you start construction on your outdoor living space, study the site carefully:

- Will prevailing winds make it too breezy?
- Will it be too sunny or shady?
- Does it overlook pleasant views? If not, consider another site or add plantings that will be pretty to look at.
- Does it offer privacy? If not, will a section of lattice or some shrubbery help?

Porches provide their own shade, but decks and patios may need a little help for at least part of the day. Here are some options:

- Permanent coverings include pergolas or latticework roofs, which provide dappled shade but no protection from rain. Solid roofs of shingle, metal, or plastic panels offer total shade and keep the rain off but will add to the cost. Whichever option you choose, integrate it with the style and materials of your house for a visually pleasing look.
- Fabric coverings include various sizes of awnings, some of which are retractable; shade tents, which consist of fabric stretched over a lightweight movable frame; and umbrellas, which come in a variety of sizes and stylish shapes and in a wide selection of colors and patterns.

A patio can be as simple or elaborate as you choose and your budget permits. You can turn the whole project over to a landscape architect, hire a garden designer to plan it and a landscape contractor to install it, or design it and build it yourself. If you decide to do it yourself, prepare for the project by learning about the foundation that will prove adequate in your climate; and to avoid ending up with a boring square of concrete, get some design ideas from photos and drawings of patios in magazines or plans books or on the Internet.

Porches

For kicking back in the shade, nothing beats a front porch. Once a staple of American life, porches are making a comeback in a big way. In fact, according to the National Association of Home Builders (NAHB), more than 50 percent of new homes are built with front porches of some kind. If you're lucky, your house already has a porch that can be rescued from neglect and made useful again. If the porch is in fairly good shape, you can revitalize it with a good cleaning, some repair to railings and balusters, and a couple of coats of paint. If it is sagging and slumping, however, it'll need to be shored up, reattached, and slightly slanted away from the building so that rainwater drains off. These are not jobs for most do-it-yourselfers. Call a reliable remodeling contractor or carpenter in your area.

Adding a new porch or replacing a decrepit one will require a larger investment of time and money, but you may find it a very worthwhile project. It will give you many hours of pleasure, add architectural distinction to your house, and increase its value at resale time.

OPPOSITE
This curvy pool patio has it all—extra-wide steps for easing into the water, a little spa for soaking, and an eating area for a quick lunch.

LEFT
The homeowners furnished this front porch for comfort. If you're updating your own porch, select architectural trimwork that will unify the makeover with the rest of the house.

Most houses, no matter what their architectural style, can benefit, both aesthetically and practically, from the addition of a front porch—or a side or rear porch for that matter. An older house will recover lost charm, and a plain-Jane ranch or tract house will gain new distinction. Porches add usable living space, of course, and function as a transition space from outdoors to inside the house.

Your new porch should harmonize with the style and period of your house in scale, overall design, and architectural detailing such as columns, railings, and balusters. If you own an older Colonial, Greek Revival, Victorian, or Arts & Crafts house, which were typically built with a porch, find out what the original would have looked like by doing some research in historical records or in architecture, design, and house-plans books or magazines. If your house is Modern, a ranch, or some other style with a plain facade, anything goes, provided that the scale, materials, and detailing are appropriate. If all of this sounds a little tricky, consider consulting an architect or designer who can either design the structure for you or suggest a style that would be compatible with your home's existing architecture.

A backyard deck or patio may lend itself better to family meals or large parties, but porches are just right for intimate gatherings or peaceful solitude. Porches on Victorian, Shingle-style, or other traditional houses look just right furnished with wicker pieces, rocking chairs, or even old-fashioned porch swings. A couple of side tables and hanging baskets or containers exuberant with flowers complete the picture. For porches on Modern houses, clean-lined metal, teak, or redwood furniture would look best.

A modest-size front porch with a concrete floor and a minimum of trim will cost about $5,000 to build—more if you enlist the services of an architect. A bigger, fancier porch with such features as a wood floor, bead-board ceiling, and elaborate trim could cost triple or quadruple that figure.

smart tip

POWER ON THE PORCH

The more amenities your front porch has, the more you'll want to use it. Whether you're repairing an old porch or adding a new one, consider putting in a couple of electrical outlets along the outside house wall so that you can plug in reading lamps, area fans, or a radio. On hot summer days you might also appreciate a ceiling-mounted porch fan. Several manufacturers offer models built to endure the temperature extremes and humidity of an outdoor environment.

outdoor kitchens

Outdoor kitchens are hot. And we're not talking about a portable grill and a picnic table out on the lawn. This latest outdoor-living luxury is a full-scale, fully loaded kitchen with an adjoining dining area where you can do food-prep, cooking, eating, and cleanup. You won't have to go back in the house until it's time for bed.

If you cook outdoors often, want to get beyond basic burgers and steaks, and are tired of trudging back inside over and over to get the essentials for a meal, an outdoor kitchen is right for you and your family, especially if you live where it's warm for most of the year. Here are some things you need to think about.

smart steps
how to plan your outdoor kitchen

Step 1 BALANCE THE BUDGET

While a decent gas grill costs about $300 and a very fancy one can run as much as $4,000, the cost of a top-drawer outdoor kitchen will set you back about $15,000 or more. That sounds like bad news, but there's good news, too—an outdoor cooking zone that qualifies as a second kitchen will increase the resale value of your house, particularly in temperate areas where you can cook out most of the year.

If the top-drawer price is too rich for your blood, consider prefab outdoor kitchens that can be delivered

LEFT
This patio offers a compact outdoor kitchen complete with a sink, small refrigerator, work counter, and storage. Sliding doors close over it, protecting it from the elements when it's not in use.

OPPOSITE TOP
Tucked between two wings of the house and sheltered by an elegant shade tent, a flagstone patio offers a shady sanctuary.

OPPOSITE BOTTOM
Light a fire and enjoyan outdoor theater experience. This pre-fab L-shaped island module incorporates a fireplace and a 42-in. auto-rising and -storing plasma TV. (See the grill on page 204.)

smart tip

FIREPLACES AND FIRE PITS

As an alternative—or companion—to a grill, you may want to consider adding a fireplace or fire pit to your patio or deck. Although neither one has the flexibility of a high-end grill, it will provide heat and a pleasant glow, extending the use of your outdoor space in the cool of the evening. Be sure to ask your building inspector about regulations and permits.

and set up in a matter of hours. Choices vary from a simple 3-foot-long island with a built-in grill, base cabinets, and a countertop to a U-shape island with a grill, side burners, refrigerator, sink, ice maker, and bar seating. Prices start at about $1,000 and go up according to the features you add. One prefab model, with a stereo, DVD player, and three mini-flat-screen TVs, in addition to cooking equipment, goes for almost $30,000.

Step 2 ALLOW ENOUGH SPACE

You'll need plenty of elbowroom for this outdoor ameni-ty. Here's a simple way to figure how much. First, outfit your kitchen on paper, factoring in the space you will need for equipment in the food-prep zone (a minimum of 36 inches of work space on either side of the grill, according to many experts), for a table and chairs in the dining area, and for other furniture in the sitting or conversation area—and, of course, allowing plenty of leeway for people to move around in all of these areas. It's particularly important to establish a clear pathway for moving the food from grill to table. If you will cook

for the same number of people outdoors as you do indoors, allow roughly the same amount of space for alfresco cooking and dining.

Step 3 PROVIDE UTILITY HOOKUPS

Your outdoor kitchen will need access to electricity, plumbing, and possibly gas lines; you can save time and money by arranging for these hookups in the early stages of the project, even if you're not certain you will use all of them. Adding hookups later could strain the budget. It will be easier—and more cost-effective—to tie into existing utilities if your alfresco kitchen is locat-

LEFT
In this Southern California outdoor kitchen, there's a pro-style grill on one side of the island and a refrigerator under-neath the counter. Although the countertop is tiled, you could consider granite, which holds up year-round in most climates.

OPPOSITE
Inside this enclosed outdoor living space, fine antiques mix with opulent fabrics, garden statuary, and lush potted plants.

ed right outside the house; but if the most scenic spot or best views on your property are some distance from the house—and cooking and eating outdoors are important parts of your life—it may be worth the extra expense to extend the lines.

If you're planning an outdoor space of this complexity, be sure to ask your local building authority about building and fire safety codes. Zoning laws may limit size and locations for outdoor kitchens, and fire codes may dictate clearances between an open flame and combustible surfaces. It may be tempting to skip this step, but you risk paying a large penalty

or being ordered to dismember the whole project if you fail to comply.

Step 4 SHED LIGHT ON THE PROJECT

Extend the hours that your outdoor kitchen is usable by providing an appropriate lighting plan. You will want most of the illumination to be soft and natural, like the glow cast by a summertime full moon; but the cooking area, stairs, and pathways should receive brighter light. A landscape architect, lighting designer, or other lighting specialist can help you with a plan that provides adequate light and handsome or unobtrusive fixtures.

furnishing your outdoor space

A roomy front porch on a traditional house cries out for wicker or wood furniture, a pair of rockers, even a glider or porch swing. Depending on how you use the porch, you might also add a small dining table and chairs; and a table lamp or two will brighten a rainy day, illuminate your summer reading, and extend the usability of the porch well into evening.

Decks and patios, no matter how small, can also be furnished for comfort. There is a huge amount of outdoor furniture available for every budget—plastic, wood, glass, wrought iron, and other metals. Create an outdoor oasis with comfortable seating for lounging, a couple of side tables, and a table and chairs for alfresco meals. And instead of investing heavily in new pieces, you can update flea-market finds or old chairs you've been storing in the basement with weatherproof paint or a top coat of varnish for new life in the great outdoors. Another cost-cutting strategy: cover your own cushions with cheerful, weatherproof fabric, which is readily available these days.

Because the line between indoor and outdoor spaces is blurring, many designers now suggest that homeowners create a seamless visual flow between the two. Use furniture, accessories, and colors that harmonize with what you've got inside, they say, although they do allow that outdoor color can be brighter and bolder. Whether you follow this advice or not, do furnish decks

and patios in keeping with the overall character of your house. A cozy cottage scheme would look ludicrous on a deck outside of a streamlined contemporary house; conversely, sleek, hard-edged metal and glass furniture is too slick for a romantic Victorian front porch.

If you want to evoke the feeling of an outdoor living room, add patterned cushions, decorative planters filled with fragrant blooms, a weatherproof rug that resists fading and mildew, and favorite objects from your house or garden—a wrought-iron plant stand, a stone sculpture, or a mercury ball, to name a few examples. This kind of accessorizing is especially important if there isn't a pretty natural view to gaze at.

Make it all pretty at night, too, with tiny lights suspended from the branches of nearby trees, hurricane lamps, or candles.

smart tip

SIZE MATTERS

Crowding isn't much fun. An arrangement of furniture that encourages conversation but avoids crowding is ideal. Also, it's best to allow about 16 in. of space between a piece of furniture and the edge of the patio and deck. Take measurements of the space and the furniture you plan to buy. Draw an informal plan roughly to scale on paper, or play with various layouts by drawing scaled outlines of each piece in chalk on the porch floor, deck, or patio to see how they work—before you buy.

OPPOSITE
To enhance enjoyment of their property, the owners converted a garage to a pool house. Comfortable chairs furnish the poolside patio.

ABOVE
Patio floors can range all the way from simple to ornate. This one boasts an intricate ceramic-tile pattern.

" We wanted the enclosure to look like

EXTERIOR RENOVATION
case study

BEFORE

AFTER

When the owners bought this house in Saratoga, New York, there was a deck already in place. (See the "before" photo, right.) As decks are supposed to do, this one provided some usable living space—in this case it conveniently adjoined the kitchen—but it was essentially a charmless structure that hovered awkwardly over the backyard on stilt-like supports that looked as if they might give way any minute. A flight of stairs, also flimsy looking, connected the deck to the steeply sloping backyard.

There were problems there, too. "The yard had water issues," says the homeowner. "Most of the time the ground was a little spongy and damp; and when it rained, water ran down the slope on both sides of the house and collected in the space under deck." Before the owners could embark on correcting the decrepit deck, they had to address the water problem.

Enter Grasshopper Gardens, landscaping contractors in Gansevoort, New York, who excavated and graded the site, installed some drains and a dry well, and solved most of the water problems. Improved drainage notwithstanding, the owners realized that their site would never permit a conventional garden or even a lawn—the ground was too soggy and the slope too steep. Another problem—the yard was studded with large rocks, some too big to move without special equipment. Just as they were about to view the property as a lost cause, inspiration struck. Why not cover the yard with a second deck and build some gardens around it, incorporating the rocks? With the help of carpenter Fred Frelinghaus of Restorations Unlimited in Salem, New York, the owners built and designed a curvaceous lower deck and replaced the old rickety stairway with a graceful and solid new one that is wide enough for two people to pass simultaneously, a special request of the wife's. She also requested a landing next to one of the beautiful old trees on the property. The deck's curved shape creates a distinctive look and contrasts nicely with the angularity of the house, the upper deck, and the stairs. The decking boards, some installed at right angles to each other, add more interest. To cover the ugly, gaping hole under the original deck, the owners enclosed it in rough-cut pine and added three triangular windows and a door. "We live in horse country, and we wanted the enclosure to look like a barn with stalls for horses," the husband explains. The metal grilles on the windows are actually lengths of rebar, typically used to reinforce concrete foundations. "It was a very inexpensive way to get the horse-stall look we wanted," he says. "We bought a few lengths of rebar, and Fred cut it with a hacksaw. It cost about $12." Another economical choice was the rough-cut pine boards, "probably the least expensive way to get some wood up," the owners say. The decking boards have not been painted or stained because the owners want them to weather to a soft gray. Once the boards have attained a nice patina, a protective finish will be applied to prevent splitting and warping.

Surrounding the deck is a "river bed" garden where stones of different sizes, shapes, and colors, many of them salvaged from the rocky backyard, mingle harmoniously with the plants and keep the soil from eroding.

a barn with stalls. "

design workbook
INSIGHTFUL IMPROVEMENTS

double-decker

A faux horse-barn facade, instead of the usual lattice, screens the area under the upper deck. A rock garden borders the lower deck.

taming a slope

Wooden steps amble down the slope, top left, through the riverbed garden, to connect the front of the house to the backyard deck.

out of the ordinary

The last step on the path, far left, curves to echo the lines of the deck and forms an unusual little bridge over the riverbed garden.

inventive ideas

Combining stock materials (left) with a keen design sense, the homeowners created a unique deck and garden within the site's limitations and without spending a fortune.

BEFORE

design workbook

GARAGE FACELIFT

spiffed up

The owner uses the second story of this garage as a professional office, so he cleaned up and added style to the building's exterior, too.

squared off

The old exterior looked dated and drab. (See the "before" shot, top far left.) To sharpen the garage doors, the owner squared off the frames' corners.

low-key accents

An industrial light fixture and for-looks-only door handles and trim, top left, add modern touches that banish the barn motif.

custom paint job

A custom finish and trimwork add character to the doors. A russet-color glaze (bottom left) was applied over the mustard-hue base coat (middle left) for a mellow look.

AFTER

resource guide

The following list of manufacturers and associations is meant to be a general guide to additional industry and product-related sources. It is not intended as a listing of products and manufacturers represented by the photographs in this book.

AD • AS (Accessible Design-Adjustable Systems Inc.)
800-208-2020
www.ad-as.com
Manufactures height-adjustable furniture and systems.

Accessible Environments, Inc.
800-643-5906
www.acessinc.com
Sells handicap-accessible products.

Amana
800-843-0304
www.amana.com
Manufactures refrigerators, dishwashers, and cooking appliances.

American Standard
www.americanstandard-us.com
Manufactures plumbing and tile products.

Amtico International Inc.
404-267-1900
www.amtico.com
Manufactures vinyl flooring.

Architectural Products by Outwater
800-835-4400
www.outwater.com
Manufactures hardwood and plastic moldings, niches, frames, hardware, and other architectural products.

Armstrong World Industries
800-233-3823
www.armstrong.com
Manufactures floors, cabinets, and ceilings.

Baltic Leisure
800-441-7147
www.balticleisure.com
Manufactures steam showers and saunas.

Benjamin Moore
800-344-0400
www.benjaminmoore.com
Manufactures paint.

Calico Corners
800-213-6366
www.calicocorners.com
Designs and manufactures custom window treatments.

Central Fireplace
800-248-4681
www.centralfireplace.com
Manufactures freestanding and zero-clearance fireplaces.

Colebrook Conservatories
800-356-2749
www.colebrookconservatories.com
Designs, builds, and installs fine conservatories, glass enclosures, period glass structures, roof lanterns, and horticultural greenhouses.

Congoleum Corp.
800-274-3266
www.congoleum.com
Manufactures resilient, high-pressure plastic-laminate flooring.

Cooper Lighting
708-956-8400
www.cooperlighting.com
Manufactures lighting products.

Council of Better Business Bureaus
703-276-0100
www.bbb.org
The umbrella organization for the 132 local bureaus, supported by more than 250,000 local business members nationwide.

Crossville, Inc.
931-484-2110
www.crossvilleinc.com
Manufactures porcelain, stone, and metal tile.

Dex Studios
404-753-0600
www.dexstudios.com
Creates custom concrete sinks, tubs, and countertops.

EGS Electrical Group
Easy Heat
860-653-1600
www.easyheat.com
Manufactures floor-warming systems.

Elyria Fence Inc.
800-779-7581
www.elyriafence.com
Provides custom fences, trellises, arbors, and decks year-round.

Formica Corporation
Phone: 800-367-6422
www.formica.com
Manufactures plastic laminate and solid-surfacing material.

Garden Artisans
410-721-6185
www.gardenartisans.com
Sells decorative backyard structures.

Grohe
800-444-7643
www.grohe.com
Manufactures bathroom and kitchen faucets and shower systems.

Haier America
877-337-3639
www.haieramerica.com
Manufactures electronics and appliances, including wine cellars.

Hartco Hardwood Floors
800-769-8528
www.hartcoflooring.com
Manufactures engineered-hardwood and solid-wood flooring.

International Code Council (ICC)
888-422-7233
www.iccsafe.org
A nonprofit organization that provides a comprehensive set of national model construction codes.

Jacuzzi Whirlpool Bath
800-288-4002
www.jacuzzi.com
Manufactures luxury tubs and showers for the home.

Kohler
800-456-4537
www.kohlerco.com
Manufactures sinks, lavs, faucets, tubs, and accessories.

KraftMaid Cabinetry
888-562-7744
www.kraftmaid.com
Manufactures stock and built-to-order cabinetry.

Lucianna Samu
lsamu@samustudios.com
Provides space planning and design services.

Moen
800-289-6636
www.moen.com
Manufactures faucets, sinks, and accessories for the bath and kitchen.

National Association of the Remodeling Industry (NARI)
800-611-6274
www.nari.org
A trade association for remodeling professionals; provides educational programs as well as online information for both professionals and consumers.

National Kitchen and Bath Association (NKBA)
800-843-6522
www.nkba.org
A trade organization for kitchen and bath specialists; provides remodeling information, programs, and business tools to professionals and homeowners.

Plumbing Manufacturers Institute
847-884-9764
www.pmihome.org
A not-for-profit national trade association of manufacturers of plumbing products, serving as the voice of the industry.

Re-Bath Incorporated
800-426-4573
www.re-bath.com
Manufactures and distributes bathroom retrofit products.

Tile Council of America, Inc.
864-646-8453
www.tileusa.com
A national trade group, represents tile companies and offers information for consumers, including a handbook on ceramic tile installation.

Toto USA
888-295-8134
www.totousa.com
Manufactures bathroom plumbing products.

Velux America
800-888-3589
www.velux.com
Manufactures skylights, roof windows, and solar-energy systems.

Whirlpool Corp.
800-253-1301
www.whirlpool.com
Manufactures major home appliances.

Wilsonart International
800-433-3222
www.wilsonart.com
Manufactures plastic laminate, solid-surfacing material, and adhesives for countertops, cabinets, floors, and fixtures.

Vantage Products
770-483-0915
www.vantageproducts.com
Manufactures Elite open-louver and raised-panel shutters, custom shutters, gable vents, siding accessories, and more.

glossary OF TERMS

Accent Lighting: A type of lighting that highlights an area or object to emphasize that aspect of a room's character.

Accessible Designs: Those that accommodate persons with physical disabilities.

Adaptable Designs: Those that can be easily changed to accommodate a person with disabilities.

Ambient Lighting: General illumination that surrounds a room. There is no visible source of the light.

Backlighting: Illumination coming from a source behind or at the side of an object.

Backsplash: The vertical part at the rear and sides of a countertop that protects the adjacent wall.

Box Pleat: A double pleat, underneath which the edges fold toward each other.

Broadloom: A wide loom for weaving carpeting that is 54 inches wide or more.

Built-In: Any element, such as a bookcase or cabinetry, that is built into a wall or an existing frame.

Cabriole: A double-curve or reverse S-shaped furniture leg that leads down to an elaborate foot (usually a ball-and-claw type).

Casegoods: A piece of furniture used for storage, including cabinets, dressers, and desks.

Casing: The exposed trim around windows and doors.

Clearance: The amount of space between two fixtures, the centerlines of two fixtures, or a fixture and an obstacle, such as a wall.

Code: A locally or nationally enforced mandate regarding structural design, materials, plumbing, or electrical systems that state what you can or cannot do when you build or remodel.

Color Wheel: A pie-shaped diagram showing the range and relationships of pigment and dye colors.

Complementary Colors: Hues directly opposite each other on the color wheel. As the strongest contrasts, complements tend to intensify each other.

Contemporary: Any modern design (after 1920) that does not contain traditional elements.

Coped Joint: A curved cut on a piece of trim that makes the reverse image of the piece it must butt against.

Cornice: Ornamental trim at the meeting of roof and wall (exterior) or at the top of a wall (interior).

Cove: 1. A built-in recess in a wall or ceiling that conceals an indirect light source. 2. A concave recessed molding that is usually found where the wall meets the ceiling or floor.

Daybed: A bed made up to appear as a sofa. It usually has a frame that consists of a headboard, a footboard, and a sideboard along the back.

Dimmer Switch: A switch that can vary the intensity of the light it controls.

Distressed Finish: A decorative paint technique in which the final paint coat is sanded and battered to produce an aged appearance.

Dovetail: A joinery method in which wedge-shaped parts are interlocked to form a tight bond. This joint is commonly used in furniture making.

Dowel: A short cylinder, made of wood, metal, or plastic, that fits into corresponding holes bored in two pieces of wood, creating a joint.

Faux Finish: A decorative paint technique that imitates a pattern found in nature.

Finial: The decorative element on top of a post.

Fittings: The plumbing devices that bring water to the fixtures, such as faucets.

Fluorescent Lighting: A glass tube coated on the interior with phosphor, a chemical compound that emits light when activated by ultraviolet energy. Air in the tube is replaced with a combination of argon gas and a small amount of mercury.

Footcandle: A unit that is used to measure brightness. A footcandle is equal to one lumen per square foot of surface.

Framed Cabinet: A cabinet with a full frame across the face of the cabinet box.

Frameless Cabinet: A cabinet without a face frame. It may also be called a "European-style" cabinet.

Frieze: A horizontal band at the top of the wall or just below the cornice.

Full-Spectrum Light: Light that contains the full range of wavelengths that can be found in daylight, including invisible radiation at the end of each visible spectrum.

Gateleg Table: A drop-leaf table supported by a gate-like leg that folds or swings out.

Ground-Fault Circuit Interrupter (GFCI): A safety circuit breaker that compares the amount of current entering a receptacle with the amount leaving. If there is a discrepancy of 0.005 volt, the GFCI breaks the circuit in a fraction of a second. GFCIs are required in damp areas of the house.

Grout: A mortar that is used to fill the spaces between tiles.

Hardware: Wood, plastic, or metal plated trim found on the exterior of furniture, such as knobs, handles, and decorative trim.

Harmonious Color Scheme: Also called analogous, a combination focused on neighboring hues on the color wheel. The shared underlying color generally gives such schemes a coherent flow.

Hue: Another term for specific points on the pure, clear range of the color wheel.

Incandescent Lighting: A bulb (lamp) that converts electric power into light by passing electric current through a filament of tungsten wire.

Indirect Lighting: A more subdued type of lighting that is not head-on, but rather reflected against another surface such as a ceiling.

Inlay: A decoration, usually consisting of stained wood, metal, or mother-of-pearl, that is set into the surface of an object in a pattern and finished flush.

Joist: Horizontal framing lumber placed on edge to support subfloors or hold up ceilings.

Lambrequin: Drapery that hangs from a shelf, such as a mantel, or covering the top of a window or a door. This term is sometimes used interchangeably with valance.

Lattice: Thin strips of wood crossed to make a pattern for a trellis or an arbor.

Love Seat: A sofa-like piece of furniture that consists of seating for two.

Lumen: The measurement of a source's light output—the quantity of visible light.

Lumens Per Watt (LPW): The ratio of the amount of light provided to the energy (watts) used to produce the light.

Modular: Units of a standard size, such as pieces of a sofa, that can be fitted together.

Molding: An architectural band used to trim a line where materials join or create a linear decoration. It is typically made of wood, plaster, or a polymer.

Mortise-and-Tenon Joinery: A hole (mortise) cut into a piece of wood that receives a projecting piece (tenon) to create a joint.

Orientation: The placement of any object or space, such as a window, a door, or a room, and its relationship to the points on a compass.

Panel: A flat, rectangular piece of material that forms part of a wall, door, or cabinet. Typically made of wood, it is usually framed by a border and either raised or recessed.

Parquet: Inlaid woodwork arranged to form a geometric pattern. It consists of small blocks of wood, which are often stained in contrasting colors.

Partition Wall: A non-load-bearing wall built to divide up interior space.

Pattern Matching: To align a repeating pattern when joining together two pieces of fabric.

Pediment: A triangular piece found over doors, windows, and occasionally mantles. It also refers to a low-pitched gable on the front of a building.

Peninsula: A countertop, with or without a base cabinet, that is connected at one end to a wall or another counter and extends outward, providing access on three sides.

Primary Color: Red, blue, or yellow that can't be produced in pigments by mixing other colors. Primaries plus black and white, in turn, combine to make all the other hues.

Secondary Color: A mix of two primaries. The secondary colors are orange, green, and purple.

Sectional: Furniture made into separate pieces that coordinate with each other. The pieces can be arranged together as a large unit or independently.

Slipcover: A fabric or plastic cover that can be draped or tailored to fit over a piece of furniture.

Stud: A vertical support element made of wood or metal that is used in the construction of walls.

Task Lighting: Lighting that concentrates in specific areas for tasks, such as preparing food, applying makeup, reading, or doing crafts.

Tone: Degree of lightness or darkness of a color.

Tongue-and-Groove Joinery: A joinery technique in which a protruding end (tongue) fits into a recess (groove), locking the two pieces together.

Track Lighting: Lighting that utilizes a fixed band that supplies a current to movable light fixtures.

Trompe L'oeil: Literally meaning "fool the eye;" a painted mural in which realistic images and the illusion of more space are created.

Tufting: The fabric of an upholstered piece or a mattress that is drawn tightly to secure the padding, creating regularly spaced indentations.

Turning: Wood that is cut on a lathe into a round object with a distinctive profile. Furniture legs, posts, rungs, etc., are usually made in this way.

Uplight: Also used to describe the lights themselves, this is actually the term for light that is directed upward toward the ceiling.

Valance: Short drapery that hangs along the top of a window, with or without a curtain underneath.

Value: In relation to a scale of grays ranging from black to white, this is the term to describe the lightness (tints) or darkness (shades) of a color.

Veneer: High-quality wood that is cut into very thin sheets for use as a surface material.

Wainscoting: a wallcovering of boards, plywood, or paneling that covers the lower section of an interior wall and usually contrasts with the wall surface above.

Welt: A cord, often covered by fabric, that is used as an elegant trim on cushions, slipcovers, etc.

Work Triangle: The area bounded by the lines that connect the sink, range, and refrigerator. A kitchen may have multiple work triangles. In an ideal triangle, the distances between appliances are from 4 to 9 feet.

index

photo credits

page 1: Stan Sudol/CH **pages 2–12:** *all* Mark Samu **page 13:** Todd Caverly **page 14:** Philip Clayton-Thompson, stylist: Donna Pizzi **page 15:** Iria Giovan **pages 16–17:** Mark Samu **page 18:** Todd Caverly **page 19:** Mark Samu **page 20:** Mark Samu, courtesy of Hearst Magazines **page 21:** *both* Mark Samu **page 22:** Mark Samu **page 23:** Mark Samu, design: Lucianna Samu/Benjamin Moore Paints **pages 24–25:** Todd Caverly **page 26:** *both* Mark Samu **page 28:** *both* Mark Samu **pages 30–31:** Tria Giovan **page 32:** Todd Caverly **page 34:** Philip Clayton-Thompson, stylist: Donna Pizzi **page 36:** Tria Giovan **page 37:** melabee m miller, architect: Karen Luongo, AIA **page 38:** Todd Caverly **page 39:** melabee m miller, architect: Karen Luongo, AIA **page 40:** Todd Caverly **page 41:** Mark Samu **page 42:** melabee m miller, architect: Karen Luongo, AIA **page 43:** Philip Clayton-Thompson, stylist: Donna Pizzi **page 44:** Mark Samu **page 45:** Todd Caverly **page 46:** *left* melabee m miller, architect: Karen Luongo, AIA; *right* Mark Samu **page 47:** courtesy of Armstrong **page 48:** Todd Caverly **page 49:** melabee m miller, builder: New Outlooks Construction **page 50:** Jessie Walker **page 52:** www.davidduncanlivingston.com **pages 53–54:** Tria Giovan **page 55:** Tony Giammarino/Giammarino & Dworkin **page 56:** *left* Tony Giammarino/Giammarino & Dworkin; *right* Nancy Elizabeth Hill, architect: Mark P. Finlay Architects **page 57:** Nancy Elizabeth Hill, design:

Helen Grubel Interior Design **pages 59–60:** www.davidduncanlivingston.com **page 61:** *top* www.davidduncanlivingston.com; *bottom* Tony Giammarino/Giammarino & Dworkin **page 62:** *left* www.davidduncanlivingston.com; *right* Nancy Elizabeth Hill, design: Susan Donahue/Sawhill Custom Kitchens **page 63:** Jessie Walker, design: Workshops of David L. Smith **page 64:** www.davidduncanlivingston.com **page 65:** *left* Minh + Wass, design: Abigail Terin; *right* Jessie Walker, design: Workshops of David L. Smith **page 66:** *top* Jessie Walker, design: Workshops of David L. Smith; *bottom* Mark Samu **page 67:** *both* Mark Lohman **page 68:** *top* Jessie Walker; *bottom* Anne Gummerson **page 69:** Jessie Walker **page 70:** www.davidduncanlivingston.com **page 71:** *top* www.davidduncanlivingston.com; *bottom* Mark Samu **page 72:** *top left* Mark Lohman; *top right* Tony Giammarino/Giammarino & Dworkin; *bottom* www.davidduncanlivingston.com **page 73:** Mark Lohman **page 74:** *left* Joseph De Leo; *right* Jessie Walker **page 75:** Mark Lohman **pages 76–83:** *all* Mark Samu **page 84:** Nancy Elizabeth Hill, architect: Mark P. Finlay Architects **page 86:** Nancy Elizabeth Hill, design: Sterling Design Architects **page 87:** Mark Lohman **page 88:** www.davidduncanlivingston.com **page 89:** Tria Giovan **page 90:** www.davidduncanlivingston.com **page 91:** Tria Giovan **page 92:** Mark Lohman **page 93:** Jessie Walker, architect: Stephen R. Knutson **pages 94–95:** www.davidduncanliv-

ingston.com **pages 96–98:** *all* Jessie Walker, architect: Stephen R. Knutson **page 99:** *left* Mark Lohman; *right* Jessie Walker **page 100:** Bob Greenspan, stylist: Susan Andrews **page 101:** www.davidduncanlivingston.com **page 102:** Mark Lohman **page 103:** Joseph De Leo **page 104:** Minh + Wass **pages 105–106:** Jessie Walker, architect: Stephen R. Knutson **page 107:** *left* Anne Gummerson; *right* www.davidduncanlivingston.com **page 108:** *top* Nancy Elizabeth Hill, architect: Mark P. Finlay Architects; *bottom* www.davidduncanlivingston.com **page 109:** Jessie Walker **page 110:** Tony Giammarino/Giammarino & Dworkin **page 111:** Jessie Walker **pages 112–119:** *all* Mark Samu **page 120:** Mark Samu, design: Benjamin Moore Paints **pages 122–123:** Tria Giovan **page 124:** Philip Clayton-Thompson, stylist: Donna Pizzi **pages 126–127:** Mark Samu **page 128:** Todd Caverly **pages 130–131:** Mark Samu **page 132:** Tria Giovan **pages 133–134:** Todd Caverly **page 135:** *both* Mark Samu **page 136:** Mark Samu, courtesy of Hearst Magazines **page 137:** Tria Giovan **page 138:** Philip Clayton-Thompson, stylist: Donna Pizzi **page 139:** Todd Caverly **page 140:** Tria Giovan **pages 141–147:** *all* Mark Samu **pages 148–149:** *all* melabee m miller, architect: Dan Lincoln **page 150:** Todd Caverly **page 152:** Tony Giammarino/Giammarino & Dworkin **page 153:** Brian Vanden Brink **page 154:** Roy Inman, stylist: Susan Andrews **pages 155–156:**

Jessie Walker **page 157:** Brian Vanden Brink, architect: John Gillespie **page 158:** Brian Vanden Brink, landscape design: Horiuchi & Solien Landscape Architects **page 159:** Stan Sudol/CH **page 160:** Jessie Walker **page 161:** Mark Samu **page 162:** *both* Stan Sudol/CH **page 163:** Mark Samu, courtesy of Hearst Magazines **page 164:** George Ross/CH **page 166:** Stan Sudol/CH **page 167:** Todd Caverly **page 168:** Peter Tata **page 169:** Mark Lohman **page 170:** Tria Giovan **pages 171–172:** Todd Caverly **page 173:** Stan Sudol/CH **page 174:** *top* courtesy of Pella; *bottom* courtesy of Clopay **page 175:** melabee m miller, builder: New Outlooks Construction **page 176:** *top* courtesy of Pella; *bottom* Mark Samu **pages 177–179:** *all* Mark Samu **page 180–183:** *all* Bruce McCandless/CH **pages 184–185:** *all* George Ross/CH **pages 186–189:** *all* Stan Sudol/CH **page 190:** Tria Giovan **page 192:** Tria Giovan **page 194:** melabee m miller, design: Byford & Mills **page 196:** melabee m miller, builder: New Outlooks Construction **page 197:** Todd Caverly **page 198:** melabee miller, design: Beth Mellina **page 199:** Todd Caverly **page 200:** Tria Giovan **page 201:** *top* Todd Caverly; *bottom* Tria Giovan **page 202:** Tria Giovan **page 203:** *top* Tria Giovan; *bottom* courtesy of Cal Spa **page 204:** courtesy of Cal Spa **page 205:** Tria Giovan **page 206:** Mark Samu **page 207:** Tria Giovan **pages 208–213:** *all* Mark Samu

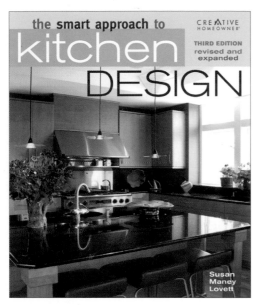
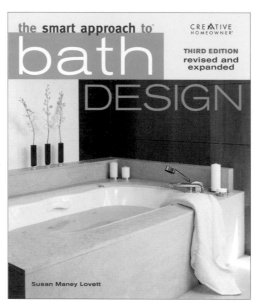